Weekends for Two in Northern California

THIRD EDITION

Weekends for Two in

Northern California

50

ROMANTIC GETAWAYS

Revised and Updated
Third Edition

BILL GLEESON

PHOTOGRAPHS BY
JOHN SWAIN

CHRONICLE BOOKS
SAN FRANCISCO

Contents

ACKNOWLEDGMENTS

The author and photographer wish to thank the following people for their contributions, inspiration, and support:

Regina Miesch, Photographic Styling
Yvonne Gleeson, Research Assistance
Jerry Hulse

Text copyright © 1991, 1994, 1998 by Bill Gleeson.
Photographs copyright © 1991, 1994, 1998 by John Swain.

Third Edition
Printed in the United States of America.

Library of Congress Cataloging-in-Publication Data available.

ISBN 0-8118-1896-9

Cover photo: The Inn Above Tide
Typesetting: Neal Elkin/On Line Typography

Distributed in Canada by Raincoast Books,
8680 Cambie Street, Vancouver, B.C. V6P 6M9

10 9 8 7 6 5 4 3 2 1

Chronicle Books
85 Second Street
San Francisco, CA 94105

Web Site: www.chronbooks.com

INTRODUCTION

Dual careers, sixty-hour work weeks, soccer, and softball. . . . Chances are it's been awhile since you and your partner stole away together—just the two of you. For us, at least, the time between getaways can sometimes be measured in months, even seasons.

Given their special nature (and infrequency), weekend trips for two are nothing to take lightly. We approach such occasions with a strategy that most would reserve for a round-the-world tour: maps, brochures, guidebooks, restaurant reviews, and itineraries, not to mention overnight babysitters and back-up overnight babysitters.

This book is intended to help minimize the element of chance that can cloud a cherished weekend for two and to help ensure that this special time away together lives up to your expectations.

Rooms for Romance

It's been several years and multiple revisions since we first set about documenting Northern California's most romantic destinations, and we've since honed our romantic criteria through visits to hundreds of inns and hotels. Our checklist includes:

- Private bathrooms (a must in our opinion; we'll tell you if any are shared)
- In-room fireplaces
- Tubs or showers big enough for two
- Breakfast in bed
- Feather beds and cushy comforters
- Canopied, four-poster, king- or queen-sized beds
- Private decks, patios, or balconies with inspirational views
- Romantic decor, special touches, and accessories
- Rooms where smoking is not permitted

We also seek out hotels and inns that exude that overall, sometimes difficult-to-describe intimate atmosphere and those that discourage child guests. While we certainly harbor no prejudice toward children (we have two of our own), many couples are seeking a well-deserved break from the kids. The (sometimes loud) evidence of little people in the room next door or in the hall doesn't exactly contribute to a passionate getaway.

Finally, most inns and small hotels have certain special rooms that are particularly conducive to a romantic experience. Instead of leaving the choice of rooms to the reserva-tion clerk and describing in detail the public areas of each establishment, we've devoted a good part of this book to detailing those particularly romantic rooms and suites. When booking your getaway reservation, don't hesitate to ask about the availability of a specific room—unless, of course, you already have a personal favorite.

Dining

At the beginning of each section, we've identified particularly noteworthy restaurants near our featured destinations. These were sampled by us and/or recommended by innkeepers whose opinions we respect. Keep in mind, however, that restaurants—and chefs—come and go. Accordingly, we suggest you balance these recommendations with updates and new choices offered by your innkeeper. He or she will be happy to offer suggestions.

A Word About Rates

While seasoned travelers might still be able to find a room along California's well-traveled highways for a song, this guide isn't for bargain hunters. Since romantic getaways are special occasions, we've learned to adjust to the higher tariffs being commanded for special rooms. In fact, most of the rooms described in the following pages start at more than $100 per night.

To help you plan your getaway budget, approximate 1998 rates for specific rooms are noted within and at the end of each description. If you're booking a weekend trip, please note that many establishments require two-night minimum stays.

Rates (per high-season weekend night for two friendly people) are classified at the end of each listing using the following ranges, not including tax:

Moderate: Under $150
Expensive: $150–$200
Deluxe: Over $200

Final Notes

No payment was sought or accepted from any establishment in exchange for a listing in this book.

Food, wine, and flowers were often added to photos for styling purposes. Some inns provide such amenities; others do not. Please ask when making a reservation whether these items are complimentary or whether they're provided for an extra charge.

Also, please understand that we cannot guarantee that these properties will maintain furnishings or standards as they existed on our visit, and we very much appreciate hearing from readers if their experience is at variance with our descriptions. Reader comments were carefully consulted in the creation of this revised edition. Your opinions are critical.

THE NORTH COAST

Daytime Diversions

If your legs are up to it, hike down the more than four hundred steps to the Point Reyes Lighthouse at the National Seashore. It's a great place to snuggle against the wind and watch passing whales some three hundred feet below.

Twelve miles north of Jenner, and definitely worth a visit, is Fort Ross State Historic Park, a reconstructed fortress established by Russian seal hunters in the early 1800s.

In Mendocino, rent a canoe at Stanford Inn by the Sea (see listing). Innkeeper Jeff Stanford operates Catch a Canoe & Bicycles Too, a rental service under the bridge at the mouth of Big River just south of the village. Big River flows through a narrow, undeveloped redwood canyon. You can rent by the hour or overnight.

Farther north, near Garberville, leave Highway 101 for a scenic, thirty-three-mile detour through the old redwoods along the Avenue of the Giants.

Tables for Two

The Olema Inn and Manka's in Inverness are good choices for travelers staying in the Point Reyes area. In Occidental, the venerable Union Hotel serves popular Italian dishes on red-and-white checkered tablecloths.

Pangaea Cafe on Main Street in Point Arena gets high marks from our North Coast innkeepers. It's ten miles north of Gualala and ten miles south of Elk.

St. Orres, the beautiful Russian-style inn located in Gualala, has a well-respected dining room that serves fixed-price dinners. Oceansong Restaurant in Gualala is also recommended by our innkeepers.

If you find yourself near the Benbow Inn (near Garberville) around dinner, try the inn's highly rated restaurant. In Eureka, consistently memorable meals are served in the dining room at The Hotel Carter.

In Mendocino, we recommend Moosse Cafe on Kasten Street, Cafe Beaujolais on Ukiah Street, and 955 Ukiah. These are within walking distance of our Mendocino destinations.

The Inn at Occidental

3657 Church Street (P.O. Box 857)
Occidental, CA 95465
Telephone: (707) 874-1047;
toll-free (800) 522-6324

Eight rooms, each with private bath. Complimentary full breakfast served at communal dining room table. Complimentary refreshments served every afternoon, and Sonoma Valley wine served every evening. Handicapped access. Smoking is not permitted. Two-night minimum stay required during weekends. Moderate to expensive.

Getting There

From Highway 101 north of Petaluma, take the Rohnert Park/Sebastopol/Highway 116 exit and follow west for seven and a half miles to Sebastopol. Turn left at the stoplight and follow toward Bodega Bay for six and a half miles. Turn right at the sign to Freestone and Occidental, and follow the Bohemian Highway for three and a half miles to the stop sign in Occidental. Turn right onto Church Street and follow up hill to inn.

The Inn at Occidental

*W*e noticed the twinkling lights of this enchanting inn quite by accident during an after-dinner stroll around tiny Occidental. We were immediately impressed.

Nestled under tall trees on a gentle hillside, the inn is a three-level century-old Victorian whose eclectic facade includes brick, balconies, and gingerbread. It served as a private home for many generations, and later it became the site of the Occidental Water Bottling Company. The building was restored and refitted as an inn in the late 1980s. Innkeeper Jack Bullard, who took over in 1994, continues to refine and improve this elegant establishment.

Rooms for Romance

One of our favorite rooms is the Cut Glass Room (around $200), a private hideaway with its own garden, patio, and hot tub. Inside is a king-sized bed and collections of antique glass and contemporary photographs.

You'll have a view of the village church from the balcony of the Tiffany Suite (mid $200 range), which also boasts a queen-sized, canopied, four-poster mahogany bed and an antique woodburning fireplace.

A large spa for two awaits inside the cozy Quilt Suite (mid $200 range), a sunny room that holds a queen-sized pine bed, two overstuffed lounge chairs, and a fireplace.

In the Sugar Suite (around $200), a sliding glass door opens to a private patio and entry into the courtyard. Lying in the king-sized, antique pine bed, your toes will be warmed by a fireplace.

Each of the inn's rooms has a private bathroom with shower. Rates start in the mid $100 range.

POINT REYES SEASHORE LODGE

10021 Coastal Highway 1 (P.O. Box 39)
Olema, CA 94950
Telephone: (415) 663-9000

Eighteen rooms and three suites, each with private bath.
Each suite includes a wet bar/refrigerator, a feather bed, a
whirlpool tub, a coffeemaker, and a morning newspaper.
Continental breakfast included. Smoking is discouraged.
Handicapped access. Moderate to deluxe.

Getting There
The inn is two miles south of the community of Point
Reyes on Highway 1. It's a one-hour drive from San Fran-
cisco, and a two-and-a-half-hour drive from Sacramento.

Point Reyes Seashore Lodge

Olema

ost any weekend, when Tahoe- and beach-bound traffic has highways leading out of the Bay Area tied in knots, the smart money is cruising north. Driving through the lush pastures and hills of west Marin County, you'll probably encounter more cows than cars.

While funky, old burgs like Bolinas, Point Reyes, and Olema have attracted a steady but slow flow of visitors over the years, there's a new reason (besides the whales) to venture up here. Though built a century after many of the historic inns that dot the countryside, the Point Reyes Seashore Lodge was fashioned in a grand, graceful style that fits right in with its Victorian neighbors.

Tom and Jeff Harriman built the inn in 1988, hoping to create just the right atmosphere for intimate encounters. They started with a choice locale: a hillside spot that commands a view of a meadow and a pine forest. Hidden by the inn from the parking areas, the panorama is especially entrancing when it unfolds for the first time as you enter your room.

Guest rooms here are compact, but the generous use of glass makes them appear much larger. Rooms along the upper floor have either bay windows or porches, while some lower-level rooms have decks.

By the way, before setting off for weather-fickle Olema, be sure to bring clothing for both sun and fog, regardless of season. That is unless you don't plan to leave your room. In that case, only the bare essentials are required.

Rooms for Romance

It is impossible to go wrong with any of the nine top-floor rooms. However, some are particularly well suited to romance.

Room 18, the Sir Francis Drake Suite, is a split-level affair with a step-down living space equipped with fireplace and refrigerator. A spectacular clerestory bay window rises from floor to ceiling, providing a view even from the paneled sleeping loft. Placement of the spa tub allows bathers an unusual opportunity to look out under the stairs through the window to the treetops beyond. There's room for two in the tub in a pinch.

Next door, the mauve-toned Garcia Rancho Suite (room 19) is a close second, with sleeping loft, spa tub, fireplace, and French doors that open to a tiny deck. The Audubon Suite (room 17) is similarly styled; both are priced in the high $100 range.

Creek-view rooms are priced in the low to mid $100 range, while terrace rooms and fireplace rooms, which also have whirlpool tubs, carry rates in the mid $100 range.

For convivial guests, continental breakfast can be taken in the downstairs dining room in front of a rock-walled fireplace. Those seeking more privacy may load their trays with pastries, juice, fruit, and cereal and retreat to their rooms.

SEACLIFF

39140 South Highway 1 (P.O. Box 1317)
Gualala, CA 95445
Telephone: (707) 884-1213

Sixteen rooms, each with private bath, spa tub, fireplace, deck, and refrigerator. No in-room phones. Handicapped access. Smoking is allowed; nonsmoking rooms available. Moderate to expensive.

Getting There
From the Bay Area, take Highway 101 past Santa Rosa to River Road. Turn west onto Highway 116 and drive west to Jenner. Head north on Highway 1 to Gualala. Driving time from San Francisco is two and a half hours.

SEACLIFF

Gualala

*E*ven with music playing softly, we could hear the not-so-distant nighttime surf pounding the Gualala beach. Add a flickering fire and you've got the fixings for a sensual feast that's well worth the two-and-a-half-hour drive from the Bay Area. The inn's sixteen rooms are spread among four clusters perched on a steep bluff overlooking the Pacific Ocean and the Gualala River. (The river separates the inn from the beach, so the seashore, although very close, isn't immediately accessible on foot.)

Rooms for Romance

Seacliff's rooms are compact but generously equipped. Each has a king-sized bed facing a fireplace and a small, private deck. In the bathroom, a spa tub for two sits beneath an ocean-view window. The in-room refrigerator holds a complimentary bottle of champagne. Bubblebath provides the perfect inspiration.

Although all rooms feature white-water views and similar amenities, we suggest the upper-level accommodations for a bit more privacy and a slightly elevated river and ocean vista. The second-floor rooms also feature cathedral ceilings. All are offered in the mid to upper $100 range.

BREAKERS INN

39300 South Highway 1 (P.O. Box 389)
Gualala, CA 95445
Telephone: (707) 884-3200

Twenty-seven rooms, each with private bath, ocean
view, deck, and woodburning fireplace; most with tubs
for two. Complimentary continental breakfast served
in the lobby and can be taken to your room. Restaurant. Handicapped access. Smoking is allowed in some
rooms. Two-night minimum stay required during
holiday periods. Moderate to deluxe.

Getting There
From Highway 101 at Santa Rosa, take the
Guerneville/River Road exit and follow River Road
west to Guerneville. Take Highway 116 to Jenner,
then drive north on Highway 1 to Gualala. The inn
is on the left at the southern end of town opposite
the Gualala Hotel.

BREAKERS INN

Gualala

O ne of the newest luxury hideaways on the Mendocino coast, Breakers Inn entices traveling couples with some of the most breathtaking ocean views available along the North Coast. However, views aren't the only attraction here. Breakers Inn also treats its guests to decadent amenities like fireplaces, comfortable decks, and large whirlpool tubs for two.

The four multi-tiered, dark wood-sided buildings that comprise the inn hug an ocean-view bluff at the mouth of the Gualala River. Gualala shops and restaurants are within a short walk or drive away. Those who are unwilling to tear themselves away from the inn for supper may dine at the Breakers' onsite ocean-view restaurant.

Rooms for Romance

The four rooms listed under the "luxurious spa room" category (mid $200 range) are the best in the house. In the stunning Japan room, for example, the centerpiece is an $8,000 handcrafted Japanese cypress spa. This room also has a four-poster rosewood bed and a sofa.

You can't go wrong with the inn's "deluxe ocean-view rooms" (high $100 range) either. These spacious corner units have sitting areas and beds set in alcoves with bevelled glass windows. San Francisco offers the best view, and it's furnished with a

sleigh bed and leather furniture.

The largest upper-level room is Cape Cod, which has vaulted ceilings and offers sunset views. Germany has a hand-painted blue sleigh bed and a large sitting area with a sofa.

"Standard oceanview rooms" are offered in the mid $100 range. Among these is Sweden, a sunny bluff-level room with a sleigh bed, and Connecticut, an upper-level room furnished in Shaker style with a four-poster bed.

Be aware that smoking is allowed in the California room and that three rooms have limited ocean views.

WHALE WATCH INN

35100 Highway 1
Gualala, CA 95445
Telephone: (707) 884-3667

Eighteen rooms and suites, each with private bath, fireplace, deck, bubblebath, and ice maker; eight with whirlpool tubs for two. Five units have complete kitchens. Complimentary full breakfast delivered to your room. Two-night minimum stay on weekends; three-night minimum on holiday weekends. Smoking permitted on decks only. Handicapped access. Expensive to deluxe.

Getting There
From the Bay Area, take Highway 101 past Santa Rosa to River Road. Go west onto Highway 116 and west to Jenner. Head north on Highway 1 to Gualala. Driving time from San Francisco is two and a half hours. Inn is five miles north of Gualala.

WHALE WATCH INN

*U*nlike many North Coast inns, in which doilies and antiques prevail, the Whale Watch Inn dares to be different. With its pastel hues, interesting angles, and skylights, the inn offers a fresh touch of contemporary elegance and some of this region's most intimate rooms and soul-stirring views.

Occupying an unusual, sunny, banana-belt spot of the coast, Whale Watch Inn is spread among five separate buildings on two wooded acres. A private stairway leads to a half-mile-long beach with tidal pools and sea lions. It's the stuff of which honeymoons are made. However, instead of the typical single bridal suite, each of Whale Watch Inn's eighteen rooms is honeymoon quality.

Rooms for Romance

First, the basics. Each room has an ocean view, a fireplace, and a private deck. But that's where the similarities end. Each room has its own design, flow, and atmosphere. The following are a few of our favorites, which are all offered in the mid $200 range.

The Bath Suite is aptly named. While the sitting/sleeping area is impressive, wait until you ascend the spiral staircase. The Pacific view and dual spa tub under a skylight make this suite one of the inn's most popular. If you're planning a weekend visit, you'd be wise to make your reservation six months in advance.

Crystal Sea, a second-floor room in the Quest building, offers a coastal view that, in our opinion, is unsurpassed in Northern California. While the ocean vista alone would have sufficed, guests are treated to a moon and star view, compliments of a skylight over the bed. For dessert, there's a fireplace and a two-person whirlpool bath.

Silver Mist, a split-level suite done in soft silver gray and lavender, has an elevated dual spa tub that overlooks the fireplace and bed.

Since our last visit, outdoor hot tubs have been added to the decks of the Heart-song and Lovesong rooms.

While our favorite rooms carry nightly rates in the mid $200 range (two-night mini-mum on weekends), Whale Watch Inn does offer accommodations that go a bit easier on the budget. The cozy Rose Room, for example, features a four-poster, queen-sized bed, fireplace, and ocean-view deck for about $65 less.

Coast Guard House Historic Inn

695 Arena Cove (P.O. Box 117)
Point Arena, CA 95468
Telephone toll-free: (800) 524-9320

Six rooms, each with private bath; one with whirlpool tub for two. Spa on site. Complimentary full breakfast is served at a communal table. Two-day minimum stay on some weekends. Smoking permitted outside only. No handicapped access. Moderate to expensive.

Getting There
From the Bay Area, take Highway 101 past Santa Rosa to River Road. Turn west onto Highway 116 and drive west to Jenner. Head north on Highway 1, and drive past Jenner and Gualala to Point Arena. Turn left on Iverson Avenue (at coastal access sign) and follow to inn on the right.

COAST GUARD HOUSE
HISTORIC INN

Point Arena

Not so long ago, visitors seeking romance in Point Arena had to be content snuggling in a motel along Highway 1 or in a chilly beachside tent. Today, thanks to the creation of Coast Guard House Historic Inn, this little community is now a full-fledged romantic destination.

Built by the Lifesaving Service at the turn of the century, the house once served the U.S. Coast Guard and stored lifeboats used to rescue shipwreck survivors. The nautical accents and antique furnishings sprinkled throughout the inn reflect the innkeepers' desire to keep the seaport lore alive.

A colorful garden grows the edible flowers used to garnish the hearty breakfasts served on anchorware dishes, which are from navy and coast guard ships.

Outside, the resident pets lead guests to an ocean-view spa, where on one of those memorable North Coast starlit nights, the sound of the lapping surf lulls guests into another world.

Rooms for Romance

The most romantic hideaway here is Boathouse (upper $100 range), a secluded cottage with an ocean view, a spa tub for two, a wood stove, and a private patio.

In the main house, the Flag Room (mid $100 range) boasts a queen-sized captain's bed nestled against three ocean-view, cove-side windows. Whitewashed walls, hardwood floors, and nautical antiques lend a navy flavor, while fresh flowers, a fluffy down comforter, and a cozy tub for two in the adjoining sunken private bath soften the decor. A sunny nook with a window seat and brass foot rail overlooks the ocean.

Upstairs, Surfmen Cove (mid $100 range) graces the west side of the house, offering an ocean view, an antique woodburning fireplace, and a Japanese-style tub for two in a private bath.

The inn has a secluded ocean-view hot tub.

閑静な

Harbor House

5600 South Highway 1 (P.O. Box 369)
Elk, CA 95432
Telephone: (707) 877-3203

Six rooms in main house and four cottage rooms, each with private bath; nine have fireplaces. Tariff includes breakfast and dinner for two. Smoking is not permitted. No handicapped access. Two-night minimum stay during weekends; three-night minimum during holiday periods. Expensive to deluxe.

Getting There
From the Bay Area, take Highway 101 to Cloverdale, and drive west on Highway 128 to Highway 1. Drive south on Highway 1 six miles to inn. Elk is approximately three hours by car from San Francisco.

HARBOR HOUSE

*I*mpressive is what the Goodyear Redwood Lumber Company had in mind when it built this 1916 house as an executive residence and exclusive retreat for VIP guests. Although its architectural style might best be described as craftsman or bungalow, a simple bungalow it isn't.

Wandering through the front door we found ourselves in a fabulous parlor lounge crafted entirely of redwood, with vaulted ceiling, hand-rubbed (with beeswax as a preservative) paneling, and imposing fireplace. The entire inn is made of redwood, fashioned after an exhibit at the Panama-Pacific International Exposition in San Francisco.

The inn's ocean-view dining room is the primary center of activity, as guests are treated not only to breakfast but also to dinner on a modified American Plan. Don't worry about having to make small talk with strangers, either. The proprietors of Harbor House have thoughtfully set the room with tables for two.

Rooms for Romance

After experiencing a parlor as grand as the one that greets visitors here, our expectations

were on the high side as we toured the guest rooms. While not as inspiring as the public area, the rooms are spacious and comfortable, and the ocean views rate four stars.

Rooms situated in the main house of many inns leave guests feeling like they're swimming in a goldfish bowl, but the six rooms under the Harbor House roof are quiet and private.

Among our favorite accommodations is Harbor (high $200 range), situated in a sunny corner on the second floor. A large room, it holds two queen-sized beds and antique furniture that includes an English library table. This room also features a loveseat set before a fireplace, an old-style bathroom with a shower, and a dramatic ocean view.

Beneath Harbor on the first floor is Cypress (high $200 range), a large room with a king-sized bed and a double bed, a velvet lounger, a fireplace, and a six-foot-long clawfoot soaking tub.

Four quaint, red-and-white cottage rooms, each with a fireplace, complete the Harbor House estate. Seaview (mid $200 range) holds a queen-sized bed and fireplace and is decorated with floral wallpaper and pine-paneled ceiling. Both Seaview and Oceansong offer sweeping ocean views. The Shorepine Cottage (high $100 range) has a king-sized bed and a private deck with a limited ocean view.

After you've savored the sea from a cottage deck or a guest-room window, head for the inn's gardens and the winding path that leads down to the water's edge. Along the way are sitting areas for sunning and relaxing.

ALBION RIVER INN

3790 North Highway 1 (P.O. Box 100)
Albion, CA 95410
Telephone: (707) 937-1919

Twenty rooms, each with private bath and fireplace;
fourteen with oversized or spa tubs; eighteen with
private decks. Complimentary full breakfast served
in dining room at tables for two. Restaurant and
bar. Two-night minimum stay during weekends;
three-night minimum stay during some holiday
periods. Smoking is not permitted. Handicapped
access. Expensive to deluxe.

Getting There
Albion is six miles south of Mendocino. From San
Francisco, take Highway 101 north past Cloverdale.
Head west on Highway 128 to Highway 1. Drive
north two miles to inn on left. Driving time from San
Francisco is approximately three and a half hours.

ALBION RIVER INN

Albion

*W*ho says cottages by the sea have to be old and rustic? Since we've found that most fit that description, we were surprised to discover Albion River Inn, a newer cluster of cozy, freestanding cottages (mixed with attractive multiroom units) designed specifically with vacationing romantics in mind.

The inn's architecture is East Coast–inspired, but its setting is pure California coast. The Albion River empties into the ocean here; each of the inn's twenty rooms affords views of this picturesque confluence of river and sea. Forested hills to the east provide the backdrop.

Rooms here range from the high $100 range for a room with a queen-sized bed, a large tub, and an ocean view, to the mid $200 range for a room with a spa tub, an ocean view, a deck, a fireplace, twin vanities, and a king-sized bed. The inn also operates a restaurant.

Rooms for Romance

Room 1 has a pitched roof and is equipped with a tiled fireplace that separates the king-sized bed from the bathroom. Room 5, a freestanding cottage, is similarly styled, but it also has a small, private deck. Both contain spa tubs for two.

Willow furnishings and mature, potted plants give room 4 an unconventional look. The pitched-ceilinged room is paneled in light wood and has a private deck and oversized tub.

Decorated in pretty, blue tones, room 2 is furnished with antiques, a tiled fireplace, and a tub for two. Rooms 8 and 9, located on the ground floor of a fourplex cottage, have fireplaces and outdoor decks. Rooms 10 and 11 on the second floor have corner fireplaces and oversized tubs.

Since our last visit, the inn has added four new cottages with spa tubs (mid $200 range). Each features a bed sitting area with a woodburning fireplace and a large bathroom with a spa tub and a separate shower. Windows over the spas have sea views.

GLENDEVEN

8221 North Highway 1
Little River, CA 95456
Telephone: (707) 937-0083;
toll-free (800) 822-4536

Ten rooms, each with private bath; eight with fire-places and bay views. Complimentary breakfast is served at your door in a basket or on a tray. Smoking is not permitted. No handicapped access. Moderate to deluxe.

Getting There
From San Francisco, take Highway 101 north past Cloverdale. Drive west on Highway 128 to Highway 1. The inn is a half mile north of Little River and two miles south of Mendocino on Highway 1.

GLENDEVEN

Little River

We pulled into the quiet burg of Little River on one of those sunny, spring afternoons that make you want to call the office and quit your job. After checking into your room at Glendeven, you might even be tempted to sell the house and move north. Perhaps to protect guests from such crazy impulses, there are no phones at Glendeven.

We found the inn's own brochure description of a "handsome farmhouse" a considerable understatement. Expecting a typically quaint bed-and-breakfast, we were pleasantly surprised at the spaciousness and diversity of accommodations at this coastal retreat. As a couple of travelers well seasoned in sleuthing out places of the heart, we found Glendeven to be unsurpassed in romantic perfection.

Rooms for Romance

True, there is a handsome farmhouse. The Garrett, a charming attic room with dormer windows (low $100 range), faces the bay. The Eastlin Suite, also under the main house's roof, offers a sitting room, fireplace, bay view through French doors, and a rosewood, queen-sized bed.

But the refurbished farmhouse comprises only a part of Glendeven. There are two other buildings housing delightful guest quarters. The Barnhouse Suite used to be an old hay barn until the inn's owners reconstructed it as their private residence. They have since moved off the property and made the suite available to guests. Priced at around $200 (more for four people), it has two bedrooms, handcrafted wood furniture, and a stereo system. An art gallery comprises the barn's ground floor.

Our favorite spot was Stevenscroft, a remote, four-room annex situated at the rear of the property. Upstairs, the high-ceilinged Briar Rose room (mid $100 range) overlooked the gardens and was decorated in a French country style.

We were lucky enough to spend a memorable afternoon and night in Pinewood (mid $100 range), located on the lower level of Stevenscroft. The decor was a playful country-style mélange, from beautiful displayed quilts and a copper weathervane to a wooden wedge of watermelon (partially eaten) and a suspended birdcage containing an oversized, stuffed parrot. French doors opened onto a private deck, and a cozy nook with daybed afforded a sweeping view to the distant bay. Wood arranged neatly in the fireplace awaited only a match.

On our first afternoon here, visions of a walk through nearby Fern Canyon, a stroll on the beach, and a picnic on the lawn outside were among our well-intentioned diversion options. But the room's romantic magic kept us indoors. (After all, how often do working parents of young children find themselves alone in such splendor?)

Apparently, we weren't the only couple to be lulled by Glendeven's sensual charms, as a detailed room diary described the rendezvous of scores of previous Pinewood guests. Skimming through the entries we paused at one particularly intriguing account of a visit by Chuck and Patty. Several pages (and only a couple of months) later, we found another Chuck and Patty entry—with even greater raves. Maybe Glendeven is better the second time around.

The Headlands Inn

corner of Howard and Albion Streets
(P.O. Box 132)
Mendocino, CA 95460
Telephone: (707) 937-4431

Six rooms, each with private bath and fireplace. Complimentary full breakfast delivered to your room. Two-night minimum stay during weekends; three- or four-night minimum stay during holidays. Smoking is not permitted. Handicapped access. Moderate to expensive.

Getting There
From Highway 101, drive west on Highway 128 and follow to Highway 1. From Highway 1 in Mendocino, turn left at the traffic light onto Little Lake Road, and drive two blocks to Howard Street. Turn left and follow to inn on right.

THE HEADLANDS INN

Mendocino

on't let the Headlands Inn's downtown location scare you away. With not a single stoplight except on the highway and a main street that's only about four blocks long, Mendocino isn't exactly fraught with noise and congestion—unless, of course, you count the crashing surf and circling seagulls.

The inn began life as John Barry's barbershop in 1868, and it has since served stints as a restaurant, a hotel annex, and, more recently, a private residence. Since taking over a few years ago, Sharon and David Hyman have upgraded the six cozy guest rooms. All have woodburning fireplaces and feature a mix of antiques, reproductions, and contemporary furnishings.

Rooms for Romance

The largest room in the house is the Bessie Strauss (high $100 range) on the second floor. An antique, pie crust–styled table and two wooden chairs sit before a lace-draped bay window that looks over the English garden to the ocean, offering guests a great spot for breakfast (delivered to your room). A king-sized bed, Victorian-style sofa, and sitting area complete the setting.

Guests in the third-floor John Barry Room (mid $100 range) can relax under a gabled ceiling or curl up on the dormer window love seat. The queen-sized feather bed sits under the brightly papered eaves. This room commands a spectacular ocean view.

The centerpiece of the W. J. Wilson Room (low $100 range) is a woodburning stove on a raised hearth. A private deck is just outside. The George Switzer Room (low $100 range) has a handsome fireplace and a cozy garret window seat.

For privacy seekers, the Casper Cottage (mid $100 range) is detached from the main house and comes complete with a small refrigerator, perfect for chilling a bottle of bubbly. The cottage is furnished with a four-poster, queen-sized bed, an antique armoire, two over-stuffed chairs, and an extra-long tub (bath salts included).

Joshua Grindle Inn

44800 Little Lake Road (P.O. Box 647)
Mendocino, CA 95460
Telephone: (707) 937-4143

Ten rooms, each with private bath; six with fireplaces. Complimentary full breakfast served at communal table, tables for two, or in your room. Limited handicapped access. Smoking is not permitted. Two-night minimum stay during holidays. Moderate to expensive.

Getting There
From the Bay Area, follow Highway 101 past Cloverdale; west on Highway 128 and north on Highway 1. In Mendocino, turn left at Little Lake Road (at stoplight); inn is on the right. Driving time from San Francisco via Highway 101 is approximately three and a half hours; driving all the way on twisting Highway 1 takes about five hours.

Joshua Grindle Inn

Mendocino

*I*n this quaint community, where bed-and-breakfast inns are as plentiful as seagulls, the Joshua Grindle Inn is a standout. Framed by a white picket fence and the bluest of California skies (when the fog's not around, that is), Mr. Grindle's old Victorian homestead is quintessential Mendocino. Situated on a pretty knoll a short stroll from downtown, the inn has for many years ranked among the most popular along the North Coast.

At breakfast, the innkeepers do a nice job of making guests comfortable as everyone gathers for homemade goodies at the antique pine harvest table in the kitchen, or you can request breakfast served to your room.

Rooms for Romance

Half of the ten rooms (each has a private bath) are located in the main house, built over a hundred years ago by the inn's namesake, Joshua Grindle, a town banker. Since our last visit, the main house bathrooms have undergone a makeover, adding new vanities, some deep soaking tubs, and showers. The Grindle (mid $100 range), Joshua's bedroom, offers an ocean and bay view, while the Master (mid $100 range) has a fireplace, a spa tub for two, a separate shower, and a view of the garden and trees. Both feature queen-sized beds and sitting areas.

The Cypress Cottage and Watertower buildings set privately at the rear of the grounds are our personal favorites, with rooms in the mid $100 range. Watertower I, our room for a night, occupied most of the ground floor of the tower, a replica (complete with inward-sloping walls) of the many vintage watertowers that dot the community. The spacious room was furnished in comfortable early American style with an antique magazine rack in the shape of the tower. A small woodburning stove sat on a corner brick hearth with wood stacked neatly in a tiny, antique wheelbarrow.

Watertower II on the second floor is similarly furnished, although it offers a nicer city view with a peek of the ocean. Cypress North (low to mid $100 range), part of the adjacent, two-unit Cypress Cottage and a favorite among returning guests, also features cozy early American furniture and a fireplace. Both cottage rooms have beamed, cathedral ceilings.

Stanford Inn by the Sea

Coast Highway and Comptche-Ukiah Road
(P.O. Box 487)
Mendocino, CA 95460
Telephone: (707) 937-5615

Thirty-three rooms and suites, each with private
bath; most with woodburning fireplace. Continental
breakfast served at communal table or tables for two.
Swimming pool and spa. Smoking is not permitted.
Handicapped access. Two-night minimum stay
required during weekends; three-night minimum
during holidays. Expensive to deluxe.

Getting There
From San Francisco, take Highway 101 north past
Cloverdale. Drive west on Highway 128 to Highway 1. The inn is just off Highway 1 at the mouth
of Big River on the outskirts of Mendocino.

STANFORD INN BY THE SEA

Mendocino

While preparing the first edition of this book, we heard that innkeepers Jeff and Joan Stanford had done wonders with an aging, motel-style lodge overlooking Mendocino Bay. After a personal visit, however, the term *miracles* seemed more appropriate. And the miracles continue.

While others might have torn down the existing structure and started fresh, Jeff, as if following some divine vision, began making extraordinary improvements, which have continued, even years later. The result is one of the region's most charming country inns—inside and out.

If you enjoy the out-of-doors, there are acres of landscaped and wild grounds to explore, gardens to tour, and even llamas to pet. There's a greenhouse-enclosed swimming pool, spa, and sauna; the inn also loans mountain bikes to guests and rents canoes for exploring Big River,

which is just a short walk from your room.

For those not motivated to wander, views of the grounds, llamas, and more can be had from the comfort of your own deck. And there are plenty of additional niceties—besides each other—to keep you occupied.

No expense has been spared in creature comforts here. Rooms are paneled in tasteful pine and are furnished with four-poster king- or queen-sized beds with down comforters and pillows. All have fireplaces or wood stoves, refrigerators, and French doors, and are stocked with complimentary coffee, chocolate truffles, and local wine, in addition to a selection of bathing accessories.

Rooms for Romance

While the decor varies slightly throughout the inn, you can't go wrong with any of the rooms. However, some accommodations have more dramatic views than others. For the best views of Mendocino village and bay, ask for rooms 7, 8, 9, 10, 11, or 12 on the lower floor or rooms 23, 24, 25, or 26 on the upper floor. The upper-floor rooms offer more private decks.

Since our last visit, a new building has been added with two single rooms and five two-bedroom suites. The Bishop Pine Master Bedroom here has a vaulted ceiling, a large fireplace, and a king-sized, Shaker, pencil-post, four-poster bed. Another new building houses the reception area, lobbies, a video library, the dining room, and an exercise room. Each of the inn's rooms has a remote-controlled television and a videocassette player, as well as a cassette/compact disc player. (Don't forget to bring mood music.)

Room rates range from the upper $100 range to the low $300 range.

Benbow Inn

445 Lake Benbow Drive
Garberville, CA 95440
Telephone: (707) 923-2124

Fifty-five rooms, each with private bath. Complimentary English tea and scones served each afternoon. Restaurant. Golf course, swimming, and boating nearby. Closed January through March. Smoking is not permitted. No handicapped access. Two-night minimum stay required during weekends; two- to three-night minimum during holiday periods. Moderate to deluxe.

Getting There
From San Francisco, follow Highway 101 north for approximately three and a half hours. Two miles south of Garberville, exit Highway 101 at Lake Benbow Drive. The inn is adjacent to the highway.

Benbow Inn

Garberville

After miles and miles of twisting and turning along Highway 101, the Benbow Inn emerges through the trees as the proverbial pot of gold. Designed by Albert Farr, who created Jack London's famous Wolf House in Glen Ellen, the Benbow was built in an era when remote resort hotels were considered destinations. The 1920s-era inn attracted guests who stayed for days—even weeks—enjoying golf, fishing, swimming, and boating. It offered vacationers all the trappings of a world-class resort, only on a smaller scale.

While other establishments of those days have gone to seed, the years have been kinder to the Benbow Inn. New owners have pumped new life into the Tudor-style structure, making improvements while preserving its historic grace and charm.

During the warm summer months, a dam is erected on the Eel River here, creating an old-fashioned swimming area.

Rooms for Romance

Wanting to view as many rooms as possible, we wisely dropped by during a winter shutdown. Otherwise most, if not all, the best rooms would have been occupied.

Actually, "best rooms" is a misnomer of sorts, since you really can't go wrong with any of the accommodations at this National Historic Landmark. Wandering down the halls, however, a few stand out. Room 206, for example, features a mood-inspiring red scheme with dark woods, English-style decor, four-poster bed, and shuttered windows.

One of our favorites is Room 119, a newer cottage room off the patio. This enormous room holds a grandfather clock, an eight-foot-tall hutch, wing chairs, a fireplace, a wet bar, and a writing desk, all under a pitched, beamed ceiling. Even after all of this there is still enough room for a canopied, king-sized bed.

The bathroom, a sensual work of art, holds a spa tub with mood lighting, a separate shower, and double sinks. A private deck overlooks the Eel River flowing just outside.

Small rooms with queen-sized beds are available in the low $100 range. Larger queen-bedded rooms are available for a few dollars more. "Terrace kings," our rooms of choice, start in the high $100 range. Plan on paying rates in the low $200 if you'd like a fireplace. The garden cottage is offered for around $300.

GINGERBREAD MANSION

400 Berding Street (P.O. Box 40)
Ferndale, CA 95536
Telephone: (707) 786-4000;
toll-free (800) 952-4136

Ten rooms and suites, each with private bath; five
with fireplaces. Complimentary full breakfast served
at communal table in dining room or delivered to
Empire Suite guests. Coffee, tea, or juice left outside
the rooms before breakfast. "High tea" served in the
afternoon. No handicapped access. Smoking is not
permitted. Two-night minimum stay required during
holiday periods. Moderate to deluxe.

Getting There
From Highway 101, fifteen miles south of Eureka,
take Fernbridge/Ferndale exit. Drive five miles to Main
Street and turn left at the bank building. Drive one
block to inn.

GINGERBREAD MANSION

Ferndale

Just when we thought we'd seen most every romantic guest amenity, someone suggested the Gingerbread Mansion and its toe-to-toe tubs. The idea for this creative bathing experience was hatched in the inn's Rose Suite, equipped with a single clawfoot tub and a mirrored wall and ceiling. Upon seeing the double reflection, guests began suggesting that two might be better than one. Innkeeper Ken Torbert listened, and the rest is history.

Even if you haven't visited the Gingerbread Mansion in Ferndale, chances are you've seen its photograph. The fabled peach-and-yellow Victorian facade has been pictured countless times in guidebooks, travel magazines, and architectural publications throughout the nation. However, this ornate manse—not to mention the twin tubs—has to be savored in person to be fully appreciated.

Rooms for Romance

Since our last visit, innkeeper Ken Torbert has created the Empire Suite (mid $300 range), a decadent chamber fit for royalty. It boasts a king-sized bed surrounded by Ionic columns and a large bathing area with a marble-and-glass shower equipped with multiple heads and massage jets; an oversized clawfoot tub is placed in front of a fireplace. There's another fireplace in the living and dining area of the suite.

In the Fountain Suite (low $200 range), two tubs are placed side-by-side at the center of a spacious bathroom that also features a tiled fireplace and a chaise longue. And since you can't spend all your time soaking, there's a queen-sized bed with bonnet canopy and a view of the garden and village from the bay window.

Across the hall, the Rose Suite (low $200 range) features a bedroom-sized bathroom complete with a bidet and a corner fireplace. In the bedroom, strategically placed mirrors around the ceiling rosette provide you with a view of a second fireplace—from the comfort of your queen-sized bed.

The Gingerbread Suite (mid to high $100 range), our romantic room for a night, held toe-to-toe tubs placed on a raised platform behind a white Victorian railing. This spacious room, with queen-sized bed and multiple, coordinating wallpapers, is situated on the main floor just off the dining room.

The Garden Room (mid to high $100 range), also on the main floor, is situated just off the luscious private garden and features French windows, lace curtains, a corner fireplace, and a queen-sized bed.

"The Original House" at The Carter House Victorians

1033 Third Street, Eureka, CA 95501
Telephone: (707) 445-1390

Seven rooms and suites, each with private bath; two with fireplaces; two with spa tubs for two. Complimentary full breakfast served in the restaurant or in your room. Late afternoon and evening cordial hour also provided. Restaurant across the street at "The Inn." Handicapped access. Smoking is not permitted. No minimum night stay required. Moderate to deluxe.

Getting There
From Highway 101 in downtown Eureka, drive west on L Street through Old Town to the corner of Third and L Streets.

"THE ORIGINAL HOUSE" AT THE CARTER HOUSE VICTORIANS

Eureka

*E*ureka native Mark Carter grew up enamored with the work of Joseph Newsom, designer of the city's landmark Carson Mansion, considered by many to be the nation's finest example of Victorian architecture. In fact, Mark was so impressed that after discovering an old Newsom-designed Victorian house plan, he replicated it for his own family—within sight of the famous Carson Mansion.

Over a two-year period, Mark and a three-person crew built the imposing, four-story, redwood manor themselves, following the architect's every original detail, down to dual marble fireplaces and triple parlors on the main floor. However, Mark, his wife, Christie, and their children soon felt overwhelmed by the size of their mansion, and they made the decision to convert the brand-new structure into a first-class country inn.

While many Victorians are dark by design, Mark deviated from the traditional slightly to give his structure a bright, airy look. This was accomplished by adding bay windows and painting interior walls a stark white. The extra light is especially appreciated during those sometimes foggy coastal days.

Breakfast, an afterthought at many bed-and-breakfast inns, is a masterpiece at The Carter House. Among the changing specialties are delicate tarts, smoked salmon, and eggs Benedict, along with fruit dishes, muffins, and fresh juices.

Rooms for Romance

The Carters' former living area on the second floor has become the inn's showplace suite (high $100 range), featuring a fireplace, an extra bedroom, and a bright and cheery bathroom with tiled floor and oak trim, as well as a spa tub for two. There's also a communal kitchen on the second floor where coffee is available.

On the third floor is the Burgundy Room (mid $100 range), actually a suite with a king-sized, canopied bed and private bath with a tub-and-shower combination. The oft-photographed Carson Mansion is visible from this suite. A harbor view is available from a gabled window in the Blue Room next door.

There are two rooms on the inn's lower level. One of these, the Striped Room (low $100 range), has its own bath down the hall. This is the least expensive room.

Rooms are decorated with Oriental rugs, fresh flowers, original art, and fluffy comforters, and they come with flannel robes.

The Hotel Carter

301 L Street
Eureka, CA 95501
Telephone: (707) 444-8062

Twenty-three rooms and suites, each with private bath,
telephone, and television; six with fireplaces; four with
spa tubs for two. Complimentary full breakfast served
in the restaurant or in your room. Late afternoon and
evening cordial hour also provided. Restaurant. Handicapped access. Smoking is not permitted. No minimum night stay required. Moderate to deluxe.

Getting There
From Highway 101 in downtown Eureka, drive west
on L Street through Old Town to the corner of Third
and L Streets.

The Hotel Carter

Eureka

*I*t's no coincidence that the two hostelries sitting on opposite corners in Old Town Eureka bear the Carter name. Mark Carter built the twenty-room, Victorian-style hotel after converting his own grand home across the street into a successful bed-and-breakfast inn (see previous listing). These and other properties form The Carter House Victorians, which have played host to such notables as Steven Spielberg, Holly Hunter, and Dustin Hoffman.

Modeled after a nineteenth-century Eureka hotel, the hotel displays the same attention to detail as the Carters' "Original House." Everything, from construction detailing and furnishings to the nationally recognized Restaurant 301, is first class.

While the Carters' "Original House" represents a total escape from everyday hustle and bustle, The Hotel Carter is more connected to the pulse of life. Although rooms are furnished with handsome English pine antiques and cozy fireplaces, they're also equipped with contemporary conveniences like phones and televisions.

Rooms for Romance

A selection of very romantic suites are found under the eaves on the hotel's third floor. These are furnished with queen-sized beds, original art, marble fireplaces, sitting areas, and entertainment centers with televisions, videocassette players, and compact disc players. They're also equipped with oversized, double-head showers and whirlpool tubs for two.

Our suite for a night, room 302, held a step-up, thirty-two-inch-deep spa tub for two under a window with views of the marina, the Carson Mansion, and the nearby Victorian Pink Lady, a local landmark. The queen-sized bed was placed nearby. A sitting room with a tiled, woodburning fireplace and couch was separated from the sleeping chamber by French doors. The bathroom was equipped with an oversized shower with dual spigots.

Two second-floor suites are equipped with single-sized whirlpool tubs. One of these, room 201, commands a view of the marina and the Pink Lady. The room also has a windowseat and a fireplace. Suite rates are in the high $200 to low $300 range.

Down the hall, room 204 (mid $100 range) holds a queen-sized bed and single-sized spa tub, and it offers a view of the Carson Mansion.

On the inn's first floor are several standard rooms and the Carters' dining room, one of the finest in the Pacific Northwest. Wine enthusiasts might wish to visit Carter's extensive "301 Wine Shop" (www.301wines.com/wines on the World Wide Web).

THE WINE COUNTRY

Daytime Diversions

After you've visited a few of the more famous wineries in Napa and Sonoma Valleys, turn off onto some of the less-traveled roads and visit a small winery or two. One of our favorites is Chateau Montelena on Tubbs Lane off Highway 29, outside of Calistoga. Walk around back for a look at the winery's medieval-style facade. While you're there, take a look at the spectacular Oriental garden complete with lake, teahouses, and an old Chinese junk.

The Hess Collection, on Redwood Road in the Mayacamas Mountains above Napa, blends the owner's fabulous international art collection with the art of making wine.

For a different perspective, the Napa Valley Wine Train makes brunch and dinner runs along Highway 29. A number of companies offer early morning balloon flights over the valley floor. Your hotel/inn staff can provide names of operators.

A less lofty but still stunning valley vista is served up, along with local wines, on the view deck at Auberge du Soleil (see listing).

The northern Napa Valley community of Calistoga is home to several spas and hot springs, where you can get a soothing mud bath and massage.

Tables for Two

Silverado Resort (Atlas Peak Road, Napa) features the best fresh seafood buffet we've ever sampled. Auberge du Soleil (Rutherford Hill Road) serves highly acclaimed meals with a view of the valley. A personal favorite is Tra Vigne (along Highway 29, St. Helena), offering memorable Italian specialties in a convivial, European atmosphere. Mustard's Grill (Highway 29, Yountville), despite its fame, remains one of the valley's best. In St. Helena, Showley's on Adams Street and Pinot Blanc on Main Street are also highly recommended.

In Calistoga, try Catahoula in the Mount View Hotel on the town's main street.

In the Sonoma wine country area, Madrona Manor (see listing) offers an excellent fixed-price dinner menu and wine list.

Auberge du Soleil

180 Rutherford Hill Road
Rutherford, CA 94573
Telephone: (707) 963-1211

Fifty rooms and nineteen suites, each with private
bath; most with fireplaces and tubs for two. Twenty-
four-hour room service, videocassette movie library,
swimming pool/spa (heated year-round and open
round the clock), steam sauna, exercise room, beauty
salon, tennis courts with staff pro, and massage service.
Restaurant. Smoking is allowed. Handicapped access.
Two-night minimum stay required during weekends;
three-night minimum during holiday periods. Deluxe.

Getting There
Take Highway 29 north past Napa. Drive east on
Route 128 at Rutherford; turn left on the Silverado
Trail and then make an immediate right on Rutherford
Hill Road to resort.

Auberge du Soleil

Rutherford

After checking in at Auberge du Soleil one lovely winter afternoon, we hurried straight through our sumptuous room to the private deck. There we settled, savoring the day's final hours of warm sunshine along with the splendid valley scene beyond—mustard-coated vineyards, wineries, and rolling hills. Returning to the deck the next morning, we watched hot-air balloons float above a dreamy valley mist.

This French-styled full-service inn, set on a wooded hillside just off the Silverado Trail, is one of few wine-country inns that afford panoramic valley vistas. And Auberge du Soleil was built with the view in mind. The inn's rooms and suites are spread among eleven cottages over thirty-three acres. All have private, spacious decks overlooking Napa Valley and the hills beyond.

Among the more recent additions to the inn's grounds is a half-mile-long sculpture trail with picnic areas.

Rooms for Romance

The cottages, named after French provinces, are set above and below a long driveway. The lower units—Versailles, Provence, Normandie, Armagnac, Lorraine, Picardie, and Alsace—offer unobstructed valley views and the most privacy. Rooms are styled throughout in comfortable Mediterranean/Southwest decor and Mexican tiles. Covered patio decks are private enough for lounging in the white, terry robes provided in each room. Rates during harvest time start in the upper $400 range for a standard room with a king-sized bed. A room with a spa tub for two carries a tariff in the

low $500 range. Suites command $700 or more.

Our room for a night, Versailles Eight, had a deluxe, king-sized bed. It overlooked the valley and the resort's championship tennis courts. We particularly enjoyed the fireplace's proximity to the bed. Versailles One, a one-bedroom suite, is another oft-requested room.

A subsequent visit brought us to Picardie, a spacious one-bedroom suite with a kitchen area (no cooking facilities) and a large living room. The living room fireplace was visible from our bed.

The bathrooms at Auberge du Soleil merit particular mention. Each has a large dual tub (Jacuzzi tubs in deluxe rooms) illuminated by a skylight. Some even boast sexy, tiled showers with double shower heads.

The Inn at Southbridge

1020 Main Street
St. Helena, CA 94574
Telephone: (707) 967-9400

Twenty-one rooms, each with private bath and fire-place. Complimentary continental breakfast served at tables for two or in your room. Restaurant, swimming pool, and communal spa. Two-night minimum stay required during weekends. Deluxe.

Getting There
Take Highway 29 north past Napa thirty miles to St. Helena. The inn is located next to Merryvale Winery on the east side of Highway 29, which becomes Main Street in St. Helena.

THE INN AT SOUTHBRIDGE

St. Helena

*T*he people who operate Meadowood Resort (see listing) created this sister establishment near the heart of St. Helena, within a short walk of some of our favorite wine-country shops and dining spots.

This contemporary-styled property was conceived by William Turnbull, Jr., who designed Sterling Vineyards, Cakebread Wine Cellars, and his own namesake winery.

The inn features skylights, vaulted ceilings, and French doors. Many rooms overlook a central tree-covered courtyard. The warm colors reflect the vineyards and nearby hills.

For around $25 extra, couples staying here have privileges at Meadowood's tennis courts, spa, and fitness center. Meadowood is about two miles away in the hills.

Rooms for Romance

Accommodations here are anything but fussy, and the decor varies little from room to room. Guest room walls are buttery yellow, and the minimalist wood furnishings have clean lines. King-sized beds are covered with comforters, and two chairs sit before a wood-burning fireplace. Bathrooms have tub-and-shower combinations.

Rates start in the mid $200 range. Winter rates are around $200 per night. At the time of our visit, romantic packages were being offered that included a bottle of a local

vintage, breakfast in bed, flowers, and a dinner for two at a popular area restaurant, starting in the mid $300 range.

Harvest Inn

One Main Street
St. Helena, CA 94574
Telephone: (707) 963-9463

Fifty-five rooms, each with private bath; most with
fireplaces. Two swimming pools/spas. Complimentary
continental breakfast and snacks in lobby. Wine and
beer bar. Bicycle rentals. Smoking is allowed in some
areas. Handicapped access. Moderate to deluxe.

Getting There
Take Highway 29 north past Napa for thirty miles
to St. Helena. The inn is at the edge of town on
Highway 29, which is also Main Street.

HARVEST INN

St. Helena

Queen of Hearts, Count of Fantasy, Earl of Ecstasy . . . with names like these, it's clear the creators of Harvest Inn weren't designing rooms with sleeping foremost in mind. Not that you won't get a good night's sleep here. It's just that there are so many other, er, things to do.

One of the more innocent—although pleasant—pastimes at Harvest Inn is a stroll around the grounds. Clusters of Tudor-style pods set among seven colorful, lush acres give the feeling of an English village. The intricate brick and stonework of the walkways and chimneys were featured in *Smithsonian* magazine. Cobblestone from an old San Francisco street was used to build the fireplace in the inn's library.

The use of brick is carried into the guest rooms, where expansive fireplaces are common. In Count of Fantasy, empty wine bottles left by former guests adorn the wall-length fireplace.

Harvest Inn occupies a prime spot of vineland just south of St. Helena. With neighbors like Sutter Home Winery and Prager Port Works, guests are never far away from Napa Valley fun.

Rooms for Romance

Lord of the Manor is the inn's ultimate accommodation. The sumptuous split-level suite, located in the handsome Harvest Manor House, has a fireplace on each level, wool carpeting, and a cozy, oak-paneled reading nook. The bedroom, on the upper level, is equipped with a spacious spa tub and shower. Lady of the Manor and Knight of Nights, two adjacent suites, are similarly styled. All three carry weekend rates of about $300 per night.

Count of Fantasy, another deluxe room with private patio, is decorated with pecan paneling, Persian rugs, a wet bar, and a fireplace. The Beaujolais Room (high $100 range) is billed as perfect for a "honeymoon couple on a budget." Inside are a king-sized bed, fireplace, and wet bar. The inn's in-ground spa is just outside.

Our room for a night, Chianti, was a large, oak-plank-floored room furnished with antiques. A floor-to-ceiling fireplace rounded one of the corners. (Wood was stacked outside.) A tug on the drapery sash of the sliding glass door revealed a private patio and view of the inn-owned Cabernet vineyard and the Mayacamas Mountains beyond.

Meadowood Resort Hotel

900 Meadowood Lane
St. Helena, CA 94574
Telephone: (707) 963-3646

Eighty-two rooms, suites, and lodges, each with private bath and deck; most have fireplaces. Amenities include comforters, bathrobes, bubblebath, and honor-bar refrigerators. Health spa equipped with whirlpool, lap pool, massage rooms, and exercise equipment. Tennis courts, swimming pool, golf course, and croquet lawn. Restaurants, bar, and lounges. Smoking is allowed. Handicapped access. Deluxe.

Getting There
Take Highway 29 north past Napa for thirty miles to St. Helena. In St. Helena, turn right on Pope Street. At the Silverado Trail, turn left; then make an immediate right on Howell Mountain Road; follow for a hundred yards and turn left on Meadowood Lane.

MEADOWOOD RESORT HOTEL

St. Helena

We may be hard-pressed to describe last night's dinner, but our first visit to Meadowood several years ago remains a vivid, pleasant memory. Flaming crimson vineyards against a crisp, blue fall sky; nattily dressed croquet players; the deer foraging outside our window . . .

Meadowood has been a Napa Valley favorite of ours for years, yet it continues to elude many. Tucked discreetly behind trees just above the Silverado Trail, the resort resists calling attention to itself. It's not marked by neon nor by any other conspicuous sign; you'll know you've arrived when you reach the security guard post. From there, the road winds through the woods, past clusters of cottages, the swimming pool, and tennis courts.

Although the vastness of Meadowood can at first seem a bit intimidating (we followed a golfcart-driving bellman to our remote cottage), the wooded walkways and twisting lanes shed their mystery after a leisurely, get-acquainted stroll around the grounds.

At the northern end of the property is one of California's preeminent croquet lawns. The sight of well-heeled gentry, resplendent in crisp whites, playing in the shadow of Meadowood's Cape Cod architecture, makes for a stunning, Gatsby-like scene, particularly on a sunny day. The resort also has a golf course and an on-site health spa.

Rooms for Romance

While many hostelries offer only a few rooms that are eminently conducive to romance, we haven't discovered any accommodations at Meadowood that didn't measure up to our lovers' list of criteria.

The resort has undergone considerable expansion and renovation in recent years. Recreational facilities have been expanded and many new guest room buildings have been added to the wooded grounds. Rates have also jumped.

In the central area of the resort, a number of suites are offered. These feature cathedral ceilings and skylights, and many have stone fireplaces. All accommodations

at Meadowood are equipped with comforters, bathrobes, bubble-bath, refrigerators, and blow dryers. Nightly rates at Meadowood range from around $300 to around $600.

Wine Country Inn

1152 Lodi Lane
St. Helena, CA 94574
Telephone: (707) 963-7077

Twenty-four rooms, each with private bath; fifteen
with fireplaces. Complimentary full breakfast served
at a communal table, tables for two, or in your room.
Swimming pool and spa. Smoking is not permitted.
No handicapped access. Some rooms are available for
one night. Moderate to deluxe.

Getting There
Take Highway 29 north past Napa thirty miles to
St. Helena. Two miles north of St. Helena, turn right
on Lodi Lane; inn is on the left.

WINE COUNTRY INN

St. Helena

*I*f you're a first-time visitor to Napa Valley, don't be discouraged by the anonymous, cookie-cutter hotels that seem to be proliferating faster than grapevines. Thankfully, there are a few relatively new hostelries that evoke the all-but-abandoned charm and character of yesteryear. The Wine Country Inn represents a pleasing blend of old and new.

The manor house, the main building, is an appealing hybrid of various styles. Although classic New England styling is evident, flourishes like the fieldstone walls were definitely inspired by historic area wineries.

The inn sits atop a hill surrounded by manicured gardens, trees, lawn, and vineyards. A swimming pool and spa (for those blistering Napa Valley summers) are located downslope from the main building.

Rooms for Romance

Like the exterior, guest rooms here draw some inspiration from the inns of old, with country-style furnishings, homespun quilts, and iron beds. Welcome contemporary touches

include patios, balconies, wet bars, and modern bathrooms. Accommodations at the Wine Country Inn are so varied that during our last visit about eight different rates were listed from around $100 to just over $200.

One of the nicest accommodations is room 24, comprising an entire floor of Hastings House, one of the peripheral buildings. The room has a four-poster, queen-sized bed, fireplace, balcony, a spa tub for two with a picture window vineyard view, and an alcove with its own daybed. Room 26 has a private hot tub on a vineyard-view deck.

In Brandy Barn, a cottage unit, room 17 has a queen-sized bed, small sitting room, and balcony. Room 22 has a fireplace and balcony. Both overlook a neighboring vineyard toward majestic Glass Mountain.

Room 9, located on the third floor of the main house, has both eastern and southern exposures and offers views of vineyards and mountains, as well as the lawn and pool area. Besides the inn's best view, room 9 features a fireplace and a balcony.

Three rooms have private outdoor hot tubs.

Cottage Grove Inn

1711 Lincoln Avenue
Calistoga, CA 94515
Telephone: (707) 942-8400

Sixteen cottages, each with private bath, fireplace, and tub for two. Complimentary continental breakfast served at tables for two. Handicapped access. Smoking is not permitted. Two-night minimum stay required during weekends and holiday periods. Deluxe.

Getting There
Take Highway 29 north through Napa Valley to Calistoga. The inn is located on Lincoln Avenue, Calistoga's main street, across from Indian Springs Resort.

Cottage Grove Inn

Calistoga

Not many of us can afford to own a little cottage in the wine country, but at Cottage Grove Inn in Calistoga we can at least rent one for a night or two. This charming cluster of sixteen individually themed cottages was created in 1996 by three couples, friends for years, who have concocted one of Napa Valley's most innovative romantic getaway destinations.

The inn is situated on the site of Calistoga's earliest resort created by town founder Sam Brannan. Two palm trees on the property mark the location of the original Brannan cottages, and the grove of Siberian elm trees that shade the compound are over a century old.

Enjoying a central location on bustling Lincoln Avenue, the inn is within easy walking distance to local spas, mud baths, shops, and restaurants. Walls with extra soundproofing and strategic placement of windows help keep down the noise of main street traffic.

Rooms for Romance

Each cottage features a similar studio layout in which the bed sits adjacent to a generous-sized sitting area furnished with comfortable lounge chairs and ottomans, sofas, or chaises. Each also has a vaulted ceiling with skylight and a woodburning fireplace. Each bathroom has a large shower, a deep spa tub for two, and a vanity with double sink. Other amenities include compact disc players, videocassette players, refrigerators, airconditioning, and coffeemakers. All are offered in the $200 range.

Although similar in design, the cottages feature distinctive themes sure to please any taste. In the Library Cottage, for example, natural wood tones combined with camel and blue hues create a peaceful ambience. A love seat covered in a rich tapestry fabric is a good place to snuggle, while an overstuffed chair and ottoman invite a long relaxing read—or snooze.

Outdoor enthusiasts—and honeymooners—enjoy the Fly Fishing Cottage, where hand-carved trout decorate the king-sized headboard, and bedside lamps are made from fishing creels. An antique fly-fishing rod is displayed over the bed. The inviting chaise longue is big enough for two.

Although there are sixteen different themes to choose from, many repeat guests can't get enough of the Victorian Cottage, with its rich rose-colored walls and handcrafted queen-sized headboard in a love-bird motif. There's also a down-filled reading chair and a fireside love seat.

Other units reveal their decorating motifs with names like Vintners Cottage, Equestrian Cottage, Gardeners Cottage, and Nautical Cottage.

Belle de Jour Inn

16276 Healdsburg Avenue
Healdsburg, CA 95448
Telephone: (707) 431-9777

Five cottage rooms, each with private bath, refrigerator, and fireplace or woodburning stove; three rooms have whirlpool tubs for two. Amenities include fresh flowers and robes. Full breakfast included. Smoking is not permitted. Handicapped access. Two-night minimum stay required during weekends; three-night minimum during holiday periods. Moderate to deluxe.

Getting There
From northbound Highway 101, drive past Healdsburg and exit at Dry Creek Road. Turn right on Dry Creek Road and left at the stoplight on Healdsburg Avenue. Drive one mile on Healdsburg Avenue (you'll see Simi Winery on your left) and turn right up the tree-lined drive to inn.

Belle de Jour Inn

Healdsburg

An Italianate-styled Victorian, home of innkeepers Tom and Brenda Hearn, presides over this compound of five tidy cottages, each equipped with the modern niceties necessary for a romantic getaway. The beds are even covered in crisp sheets dried by the sun.

Each morning, guests are invited into Tom and Brenda's Victorian for breakfast. Later in the day, the two (or four) of you might want to schedule a romantic, chauffeured backroad or winery tour in the innkeepers' classic 1925 Star automobile.

Rooms for Romance

New since our first visit is the Carriage House (mid $200 range), whose entire second floor is a deluxe country suite with high vaulted ceilings, wood plank floors, and antique pine furniture. There's a compact disc player, a gas fireplace, and a reading nook made from redwood salvaged from the property's original barn. A view

of the valley is offered from the king-sized, four-poster, canopied bed and from the spa tub for two, which occupies its own alcove. There's also a separate shower.

Terrace Room (around $200) holds a king-sized brass bed and a fireplace. A big spa tub for two sits under a window overlooking your private raised deck and an expanse of rolling tree-studded countryside beyond. Roses bloom out front.

The Caretaker's Suite is another favorite. A king-sized bed dominates one end of this spacious room, which has hardwood floors and a sitting area with wicker furniture. A fireplace is close enough to warm your toes under the sheets. This room, which also has a whirlpool tub for two and a separate shower, is priced at around $200.

Atelier is a large sunny studio with a vaulted ceiling, woodburning stove, a queen-sized, canopied bed, and a whirlpool tub for one. The Morning Hill Room has a French-door entry, a queen-sized bed, and a shower and steam unit in the bathroom. These two rooms are offered in the low to mid $100 range.

Madrona Manor

1001 Westside Road
Healdsburg, CA 95448
Telephone: (707) 433-4231

Twenty-one rooms and suites, each with private bath; eighteen with fireplaces. Swimming pool. Restaurant. Complimentary full breakfast served in the restaurant or in your room. Modified American plan available on request. Smoking is not permitted. Handicapped access. Two-night minimum stay required during weekends. Moderate to deluxe.

Getting There
From Highway 101, take the Central Healdsburg exit at Westside Road and drive west to inn. Healdsburg is sixty-five miles north of San Francisco.

MADRONA MANOR

Healdsburg

It's difficult to believe (for this working couple, anyway) that the three-story elegance of Madrona Manor was originally intended to be only a summer retreat. Although wealthy San Francisco businessman John Paxton enjoyed the mansion for a time, the home actually stood vacant for nearly half its hundred years, until 1981. That's when John and Carol Muir arrived on the scene with visions of creating an inn. The couple's diligence has paid dividends as Madrona Manor has emerged as one of Northern California's pre-eminent country inns.

The buildings are spread over eight landscaped acres. Offering a total of twenty-one rooms and suites, the inn is large compared to many of its Victorian counterparts. Nine guest rooms are found in the manor house, with the rest housed in the Carriage House (nine rooms; six with fireplaces), the Meadow Wood complex (two suites), and the Garden Cottage.

Rooms for Romance

Wedding nights are often spent in room 204 (around $200), a front-facing hideaway in the manor house. Once the bedroom of the original owner, room 204 is still equipped with original furnishings from a century ago. A bay window overlooks the gardens and fountain, and the balcony has a pair of chairs for savoring the Dry Creek Valley. The bathroom has a clawfoot tub.

We do not recommend rooms 301 or 302 in the manor house for a romantic getaway.

Suite 400 (mid $200 range), located in the Carriage House, is an elegant hideaway with a private deck. The bathroom, boasting green Grecian tile, holds a spa tub for two. Shutters above the tub open to reveal the suite's tiled fireplace. Room 401 in the Carriage House has a rate in the mid $100 range and is a favorite among lovers on a budget.

More modern decor is found in the Garden Cottage (low $200 range), a spacious and secluded retreat equipped with a marble fireplace, tub for two, and private deck.

SAN FRANCISCO AND THE BAY AREA

Daytime Diversions

At Stow Lake (in the heart of Golden Gate Park), the two of you can rent a paddleboat for your own private cruise. The trail around the lake is perfect for a quiet stroll. The park's Japanese Tea Garden (near the lake and art museums) is another romantic spot. You'll follow delicate paths past a teahouse, pagoda, and ponds and over intricate bridges. The cherry blossoms bloom in spring, making the Tea Garden a special place to visit.

If you'd like to leave the crowds behind, board the Tiburon ferry for a trip to Angel Island in San Francisco Bay. You can bring your bikes on the ferry, and the island offers great private picnicking possibilities and enchanting city views.

Tables for Two

For a before- or after-dinner drink with a romantic San Francisco view, try Club 36 on top of the Grand Hyatt Hotel on Union Square, or McCormick & Kuleto's in Ghirardelli Square, which overlooks Aquatic Park, historic ships, the bay, and the Golden Gate Bridge.

For dinner in the city, we can recommend Vivande Ristorante in Opera Plaza and Rose Pistola on Columbus Avenue for Italian food. Slanted Door on Valencia Street wins raves for its Vietnamese dishes. Another San Francisco top choice is Postrio, Wolfgang Puck's award-winning restaurant on Post Street.

Mikayla, the restaurant at Casa Madrona (see listing), is a romantic favorite in Sausalito. Local innkeepers also recommend the nearby Angelinos on Bridgeway in Sausalito.

In Half Moon Bay, try Pasta Moon. In Princeton-by-the-Sea, our innkeepers recommend the Shore Bird.

ARCHBISHOPS MANSION INN

1000 Fulton Street
San Francisco, CA 94117
Telephone: (415) 563-7872;
toll-free (800) 543-5820

Fifteen rooms and suites, each with private bath; eleven with fireplaces, three with tubs for two. Complimentary continental breakfast delivered to your room on a silver tray. Smoking is allowed in the dining room only. No handicapped access. Two-night minimum stay required during weekends. Moderate to deluxe.

Getting There
Take Ninth Street exit from Highway 101 north; cross Market Street onto Larkin Street, left on Hayes Street, right onto Steiner, two blocks north to Fulton.

ARCHBISHOPS MANSION INN

San Francisco

*E*arly during a visit to the stately Archbishops Mansion, our traveling companions joked about whether a suitable romantic mood could be kindled in a dwelling that over the years had hosted a procession of priests, nuns, and high-ranking Catholic officials.

The next morning, we asked one of our friends if the inn's religious history had cooled their evening. "Not at all," he noted, shooting a knowing wink at his wife. "We would have made the archbishop blush."

Indeed, the inn's former residents and visitors would be more than a little shocked at the antics that take place behind closed doors here these days, what with cozy fireplaces, canopied beds, and the like. Other than the name, not much remains to remind visitors of the inn's interesting past.

The spartan furnishings of yesteryear (the mansion housed a succession of archbishops over a period of some forty years) have given way to a trove of beautiful objets d'art, antiques, and other pieces, including Noel Coward's grand piano and an elaborate chandelier that reportedly made an appearance in *Gone with the Wind*. Guest rooms, nicely updated while maintaining period charm, are also decorated with handsome furnishings dating back to the nineteenth century.

And don't forget to take a walk to the top of the hillside square for one of San Francisco's most often photographed views: the row of colorful Victorian "painted ladies" over which the stunning city skyline looms.

Rooms for Romance

We sampled Traviata, a first-floor, two-room corner suite. The sitting room held a small fireplace with mirrored mantle and several antiques and was illuminated by several sunny windows. The bedroom, accessible only through the bathroom, held two full-sized beds.

The Gypsy Baron (high $200 range) is the inn's honeymoon suite, with a large fireplace and tub for two. Double spa tubs are also found in the Der Rosenkavalier and Romeo and Juliet rooms (around $200). In the ultimate Don Giovanni Suite (high $300 range), originally the archbishop's room, guests are treated to a large parlor, two fireplaces, and an antique bed from a French castle. The second-floor Carmen Suite (mid $200 range) features an expansive bathroom with a clawfoot tub and its own fireplace.

Romantics on a budget may sample a couple of cozy rooms with canopied beds priced in the low to mid $100 range.

THE MAJESTIC

1500 Sutter Street (at Gough)
San Francisco, CA 94109
Telephone: toll-free (800) 869-8966

Fifty-nine rooms and suites, each with private bath;
many with gas fireplaces and clawfoot soaking tubs
(with shower). Restaurant. Valet parking. No handicapped access. Smoking is allowed. Moderate to
deluxe.

Getting There
From Highway 101, take the Ninth Street exit.
Cross Market Street onto Larkin Street, turn right
on Franklin Street, and drive several blocks north
past Sutter. Turn left on Pine Street and left on Gough
Street. Hotel is on the corner of Sutter and Gough
Streets.

THE MAJESTIC

San Francisco

*T*hey say you'll find a city's best restaurant by asking where the locals eat. As we discovered, this is a pretty good method for locating a romantic hotel. At The Majestic, an early-1900s mansion-turned-hotel, you're not likely to run into too many tourists sporting "I Love San Francisco" T-shirts. According to the management, this hotel is a favorite among Bay Area folks looking for a weekend getaway in the city.

Outside, the stately Edwardian facade hasn't changed much over the years. And while the interior was all but gutted during a major renovation, the decor, from rich, hand-milled English carpeting to twinkling chandeliers, is true to the earlier era.

Although we're usually anxious to settle into our room, we poked around The Majestic's lobby area before checking in. We followed the convivial conversation in the hotel cafe, whose horseshoe-shaped bar came from an old Parisian bistro. Around the bar hangs an unusual collection of butterflies from all over the globe.

The Majestic is over ten blocks from the Union Square shopping area, but we gladly surrendered the car upon arrival (the hotel provides valet parking) and found public transportation and walking to be enjoyable, functional alternatives. In the daytime, Union Square is a pleasant, invigorating walk, or a short ride away in the hotel limousine shuttle offered twice each weekday morning. At night, cab fare to the theater district is less than what it would cost to park the car.

Rooms for Romance

As he turned the key to room 403, our bellman shot us a wink. "This is my favorite room," he said. While we might have suspected he would heap similar praise on a basement room next to the boiler, it was immediately obvious he wasn't just hankering for a big tip. Sunlight streamed through the five-window, corner bay, and a four-poster, canopied, queen-sized bed sat in the middle of the red-hued room. A gas fireplace flickered in one corner. The bellman, who'd led many couples to this romantic hideaway before, was quickly on his way.

Although each room at The Majestic is styled differently, the layout and decor of room 403 (a grand deluxe room) is similar to that found in rooms 203 and 303. All are offered in the high $100 range. Not being accustomed to street noise, we worried that the traffic on Gough Street might keep us awake at night. It didn't. If quiet is important, however, room 512—facing less noisy Sutter Street—is a good choice.

On a more recent visit, we were assigned room 207, known as the Herb Caen Suite (high $200 range), a spacious retreat named after the late *San Francisco Chronicle* newspaper columnist. The sitting room, which featured a bay window and a gas fireplace with a carved mantle, held a couch, a chair, and a desk. In the bed chamber was a partially canopied, four-poster, king-sized bed.

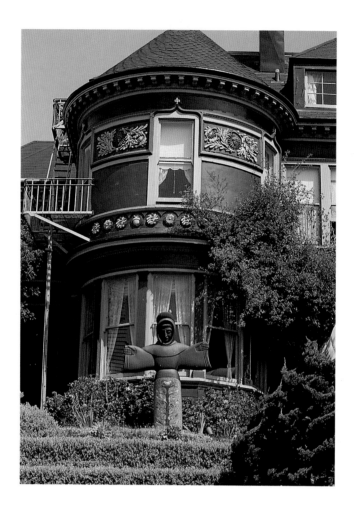

THE MANSIONS

2220 Sacramento Street
San Francisco, CA 94115
Telephone: (415) 929-9444

Twenty-one rooms and suites, each with private bathroom; some with woodburning stoves or fireplaces.
Complimentary full breakfast served in the restaurant.
Magic shows every night. Smoking is allowed. No
handicapped access. Moderate to deluxe.

Getting There
From Highway 101 north in San Francisco, take
Sixth Street exit; cross Market Street and continue
onto Taylor Street. Follow Taylor to Sacramento
Street; turn left, eleven blocks to hotel on Sacramento
and Buchanan.

THE MANSIONS

San Francisco

The setting is a prim and proper mansion in San Francisco's most exclusive neighborhood. But what's this? Blazing wall murals of picnicking and pool-shooting pigs? A caged macaw and cooing doves? The saw-playing innkeeper performing in the parlor? Hardly what you'd expect to find in staid Pacific Heights.

While we foreswore applying the abused and overused word *unique* to any of the descriptions in this book, the Mansions left me no choice. It's likely the most unique overnight adventure you'll hope to experience in Northern California.

We must admit, the term *garish* also came to mind upon stepping into the grand foyer. But after adjusting to the visual overload, we began exploring, with anticipation, the myriad parlors and hallways, wondering what on earth we'd discover next. There are whimsical objets d'art with a predominating pig theme (the innkeeper calls this "porkabilia"), millions of dollars worth of museum-quality works of art including mosaics and sculptures by Bufano, and magnificent Victorian ornaments.

Rooms for Romance

The high-spirited themes of the public rooms are carried, with gusto, into guest chambers. Among the unusual touches are walls emblazoned with murals paying tribute to folks associated with San Francisco history and lore. For example, Mrs. Charles Crocker, wife of the railroad czar, overlooks the Crocker Room, a bay-windowed, second-floor room with queen-sized bed and red carpet.

A favorite among brides (many weddings take place here) is the outlandishly styled Empress Josephine room (low to mid $200 range), with Louis XIV antique furnishings, including the largest armoire we've ever seen. French doors open to a large, private, front-facing balcony, and the bath has a window that overlooks the rear garden. Entry to the opulent room is via the hotel's restaurant, up a private set of stairs.

Around back, off the garden, is the privately situated Celebrity Suite (around $200). Inside is an unusual and tasteful combination of Oriental and American antiques, a queen-sized brass bed, and a woodburning stove. This room has the most romantic bath, decorated in black and equipped with a big spa tub and wet bar.

The hotel expanded in recent years with the acquisition of the mansion next door, an inn formerly known as the Hermitage House. A foyer now connects the two. The new addition, referred to as the West Wing, features accommodations sporting more traditional, country decor.

Among the rooms here is the front-facing, yellow-and-white Master Bedroom (high $100 range) on the second floor, equipped with a king-sized bed and a fireplace. The bathroom has a clawfoot tub into which the two of you might be able to squeeze, in a pinch.

Romantic travelers should be aware that accommodations classified as small guest rooms (low to mid $100 range) have a detached bathroom. You might consider spending a little more for a larger room or even a suite here. After all, just think what you'll save on San Francisco museum admission and entertainment tickets. It's all here.

PETITE AUBERGE

863 Bush Street
San Francisco, CA 94108
Telephone: (415) 928-6000;
toll-free (800) 365-3004

Twenty-six rooms, each with private bath; seventeen with gas fireplaces.
Complimentary full buffet breakfast served at tables for two in dining
room; served in your room for extra charge. Smoking is not permitted.
No handicapped access. Moderate to deluxe.

Getting There
From Highway 101 north, take the Sixth Street exit. Cross Market Street
onto Taylor Street, turn east (right) on Bush; inn is immediately on your
right, two and a half blocks from Union Square, between Mason and
Taylor Streets.

Petite Auberge

San Francisco

*I*t took only one visit to a downtown, high-rise chain hotel to convince us never to do it again. This city is just too special and our time alone too fleeting to settle for a forgettable night in some big anonymous box.

Only a stone's throw from those hulking, big names of the hotel industry, Petite Auberge, with its delicately ornate, Baroque design and curved bay windows, has established quite a reputation among those of us who think small. What it lacks in its number of rooms, this little French country retreat more than makes up for in charm and comfort.

Rooms for Romance

On the second floor, placed at the back of the inn, far from any traffic noise, room 26 (mid $100 range) is classified as a large room. Like the rest of the hostelry, it's done in a French country theme. This room is furnished with reproduction antiques, queen-sized bed, armoire, bookshelves, an old writing desk, and gas fireplace. The tiled bathroom holds a pedestal sink and tub-and-shower combination. Room 56 has a similar configuration, but is on the fifth floor.

A bit more compact is room 25 (mid $100 range), with two large windows (side-facing; no view), a fireplace with carved and painted mantlepiece, and a queen-sized bed.

The charming, front-facing rooms (31, 41, and 51) feature cozy window seats in the curved bays, whose windows have been double paned to reduce noise from busy Bush Street. Rates for these rooms are in the mid $100 range.

Our favorite room is 10, the Petite Suite. Reached by a very private outdoor walkway off the dining-room area, the suite (low $200 range) features lace curtains, the inn's only king-sized bed, wet bar, refrigerator, fireplace, television, videocassette player, and lots of shelves with country-style knicknacks. The bathroom has a rather compact spa tub, into which both of you might be able to squeeze. French doors open to the suite's private, sunny redwood deck.

The White Swan Inn

845 Bush Street
San Francisco, CA 94108
Telephone: (415) 775-1755;
toll-free (800) 999-9570

Twenty-six rooms, each with private bath and gas fireplace. Complimentary full buffet breakfast served at tables for two in the dining room. Smoking is not permitted. No handicapped access. Moderate to deluxe.

Getting There
From Highway 101, take the Sixth Street exit. Cross Market Street onto Taylor Street, turn east (right) on Bush Street. The inn is between Mason and Taylor Streets on the right, two and a half blocks from Union Square and one and a half blocks to Powell Street cable car line.

THE WHITE SWAN INN

San Francisco

*M*embers of the Post family, who operate several other Northern California inns, including the Petite Auberge located next door, apparently couldn't rest until giving San Francisco visitors yet another romantic lodging alternative with their tasteful renovation of an early 1900s-era hotel.

The White Swan Inn draws its inspiration from the inns of old England. The library and living room—with well-stocked bookshelves, flickering fireplaces, and handsome English antiques in rich, warm woods—will make you feel more like a tourist in London than San Francisco.

Rooms for Romance

Rooms at the White Swan are differentiated not so much by amenities and decor—they're each equipped with a gas fireplace, a wet bar, a private bathroom, and attractive furnishings—but by bed and room size.

Room 44 (mid $100 range) on the fourth floor is a queen-bed room. It faces the side of the hotel and features a nice bay with window seat, although without a view. The

bathroom is small but manages to include all the necessities.

While we found the queen-bed rooms adequate in size, the king-bed rooms, offered for about $20 more, are larger still. For instance, room 47 has a separate dressing area with a sink. The windows in this sunny room comprise almost an entire wall (with no view to speak of). This and the other king-bed rooms whose numbers end with a 6 or 7 all face the back of the property and are among the most quiet.

Since our first visit, the inn has created three honeymoon suites ($200 to mid $200 range) with canopied beds and refrigerators stocked with complimentary gourmet chocolates and a bottle of champagne.

PILLAR POINT INN

380 Capistrano Road
Princeton-by-the-Sea, CA
Mailing address: P.O. Box 388
El Granada, CA 94018
Telephone: (415) 728-7377

Eleven rooms, each with ocean/harbor view, private bath, fireplace, VCR, refrigerator, and feather bed. Complimentary full breakfast served in dining room. Smoking is not permitted. Handicapped access. Two-night minimum stay required during weekends and holiday periods. Expensive.

Getting There
From Highway 1, four miles north of Half Moon Bay, drive west (toward ocean) into the harbor area at Capistrano Road to inn.

PILLAR POINT INN

Princeton-by-the-Sea

*W*e had traveled the scenic Highway 1 route between Santa Cruz and San Francisco dozens of times, but it wasn't until Pillar Point Inn opened that we realized there was such a place as Princeton-by-the-Sea.

If you're seeking a destination resort or city, this sleepy community won't even make the list. However, as a cozy stopover or an alternative romantic getaway spot that's quickly accessible (less than one hour) from most anywhere in the Bay Area, Pillar Point Inn fits the bill.

The contemporary, New England–style hostelry overlooks bustling Pillar Point Harbor on the ocean side of the San Francisco peninsula, just four miles north of Half Moon Bay and about twenty-five miles south of San Francisco.

When creating the establishment just a few years ago, Pillar Point's builders could easily have followed the California hotel crowd and aimed for quantity. Instead, they chose not to ruin a good thing, and the inn's size was held to only a few cozy rooms.

Rooms for Romance

With only eleven guest rooms to furnish, the inn could afford to splurge. Each room is equipped with antique reproductions (down to the radio and refrigerator), a VCR, a tiled fireplace, and a brass-and-porcelain feather bed. All but one have window seats that overlook the harbor.

Although ground-level rooms feature enclosed tubs that convert to steam baths, a second-floor room offers a bit more distance from busy Capistrano Road, which runs in front of the inn. Double-paned windows do keep the traffic noise down, but passing cars can be heard when windows are open to take advantage of ocean breezes.

Decor doesn't vary much from room to room, but rooms 6 and 10, both second-floor end units, have Palladian-style arched windows and a touch more privacy (neighbors on only one side). Room 11 is slightly bigger and contains a king-sized bed.

Rates at Pillar Point Inn are in the mid to upper $100 range.

Cypress Inn on Miramar Beach

407 Mirada Road
Half Moon Bay, CA 94019
Telephone: (415) 726-6002;
toll-free in California: (800) 832-3224

Twelve rooms, each with private bath, fireplace, and ocean-view deck. Complimentary full breakfast and afternoon tea included. Smoking is not permitted. Handicapped access. Two-night minimum stay required during weekends, excluding Friday nights. Expensive to deluxe.

Getting There
From Highway 1, twenty-six miles south of San Francisco, turn west onto Medio Avenue and follow to inn on the corner of Medio and Mirada.

CYPRESS INN ON MIRAMAR BEACH

Half Moon Bay

For the folks who run Cypress Inn on Miramar Beach, a beautiful but off-the-beaten-track location is a mixed blessing. Although they don't get too many drive-bys, guests who have discovered this contemporary hideaway enjoy not only solitude but quick access (a dozen steps) to a five-mile stretch of white sandy beach.

Mexican folk art is the unusual theme here, and it's carried through from food to furnishings. When we dropped in one afternoon, the staff had just assembled a midday snack with wine in the dining area on the ground floor.

Rooms for Romance

El Sol (around $200), a sunny, lower-level corner room, is painted a bold yellow and decorated with wooden pillars, a tiled fireplace, and live cacti. On the second floor, El Viento beckons with a warm, pink theme.

Las Nubes (upper $200 range), the third-floor penthouse suite, is the inn's largest and most romantic room, featuring magnificent ocean views, large private deck, a cushy sofa near the fireplace, and spa tub for two. One room is offered in the $150 range, although most carry rates in the mid to high $100 range.

Since our first visit, the inn has added four rooms, each with a luxurious spa tub for two and fireplace. These range from the upper $100 range to the mid $200 range.

Each room at Cypress Inn features terra-cotta tile floors (with radiant heat), a comforter, down pillows, a fireplace, a writing desk, and a small sundeck. All have ocean views.

East Brother Light Station

117 Park Place
Point Richmond, CA 94801
Telephone: (510) 233-2385

Four rooms, one with shower/tub. Dinner and breakfast included. Open Thursday through Sunday. Smoking is not permitted. No handicapped access. Deluxe.

Getting There
Guests are transported by boat to the island from
Point San Pablo Yacht Harbor on the Richmond side
of the bay in Contra Costa County. The innkeepers
will send a map with confirmation.

EAST BROTHER LIGHT STATION

Point Richmond

*G*etting away from it all" takes on a whole new meaning when you're sleeping on a one-acre island a quarter-mile out in San Francisco Bay. Except for (no more than) three other couples, an innkeeper, and resident gulls, it's just the two of you. One of the oldest establishments listed in our guide, East Brother Light Station was built in 1873 and is the oldest of all the West Coast lighthouses still in operation. That's right. The old beacon still sweeps the bay and the fog horn still blows from October through March. Guests can even wander up the tower stairs for a close look at the powerful working lens.

The light station was tended by keepers for much of its history, but the facilities went downhill after the Coast Guard automated the signals in 1969. A decade later, a nonprofit group was organized to restore and preserve the station for public use, and overnight visitors soon followed.

Since you can't come and go at will, guests are treated to a sumptuous, four-course dinner, complete with wine, as well as a hot breakfast. At the time of our travels, cost per couple, per night was around $300, including meals.

It's important to note that only one room, the Marin, has a private shower/bathtub, and it can only be used if you're visiting for more than one night. Water, which is collected in a cistern from winter rains, is usually in short supply. Basins, however, are provided in two rooms.

Rooms for Romance

The Marin Room is on the second floor and—like the other three rooms here—is decorated with antique furniture and Laura Ashley fabrics. On a clear day, Mount Tamalpais and the Marin County coast are visible from your queen-sized brass bed. This is the room most favored by visiting honeymoon couples.

The San Francisco Room, so-named for the glorious view of the city afforded from its windows, is furnished in similar decor with a queen-sized bed. The small bath in this room does not have bathtub/shower facilities. Be advised that the downstairs rooms share a bathroom with tub and shower.

If the solitude of your lighthouse room gets to be too overwhelming, there's always dinner, when the other guests (if there are any) gather in the dining room for the candlelight evening meal.

A final note: Make sure you eat your fill at dinner. If you get a craving for a Big Mac later on, it's a long swim.

Casa Madrona Hotel

801 Bridgeway
Sausalito, CA 94965
Telephone: (415) 332-0502

Thirty-four rooms and suites, each with private bath;
sixteen have fireplaces and four have tubs for two.
Restaurant. Spa. Complimentary continental breakfast
served in restaurant or in your room. Handicapped
access. Smoking is not permitted. Two-night minimum
stay required during weekends. Moderate to deluxe.

Getting There
From Highway 101 north, exit at Alexander Avenue,
and follow to Bridgeway. From Highway 101 south,
take Marin/Sausalito exit to Bridgeway.

CASA MADRONA HOTEL

Sausalito

Choosing a romantic room at Casa Madrona is like making a selection from the menu of a four-star restaurant. It'll make you hungry, but you'll definitely have trouble deciding. To make it a tiny bit easier, the good folks here have added little asterisks to the room menu alongside the names of ten rooms "particularly suited for honeymoons or other special occasions." They know what we're looking for.

This enchanting hotel is draped over a green, Sausalito hillside overlooking San Francisco Bay, and most of the rooms are situated to take full advantage of this inspiring setting.

Rooms for Romance

At the top of the hill is the Victorian House, a stately old mansion that for many years comprised the entire inn. Among the dozen rooms in the manor house is La Salle (mid to upper $100 range), decorated in a French country style and complemented by a dual spa tub. The Belle Vista Suite (high $100 range) offers a romantic San Francisco skyline view and a freestanding tub for two in the living room.

The gabled and balconied rooms of the New Casa sweep artfully down the hillside below the manor house. Rooms here are modern and come in many shapes, sizes, and styles. In the mid to upper $100 range is Kathmandu, where huge cushions encourage lounging and tiny nooks invite exploring. A fireplace and tub for two complete this room.

Also worth noting are the Rose Chalet (high $100 range)—with its pine furniture, separate bed alcove, fireplace, deck, and view—and the Renoir Room (upper $100 range), where guests luxuriate in a clawfoot tub surrounded by a garden mural. There's also a window seat, fireplace, and deck from which to enjoy a spectacular bay view.

Three cottages complete the Casa Madrona complex. La Tonnelle, for example, is offered in the mid to upper $100 range and features a woodburning stove, king-sized bed, bay view, and private patio. The hotel describes this retreat as the greatest hideout in Sausalito.

The Inn Above Tide

30 El Portal
Sausalito, CA 94965
Telephone: (415) 332-9535

Thirty rooms, each with private bath and tub for two; twenty-two with woodburning or gas fireplace. Complimentary continental breakfast served at communal table, tables for two, or in your room; complimentary wine served in the evening. Handicapped access. Smoking is not permitted. Two-night minimum stay required during weekends and holiday periods. Deluxe.

Getting There
From Highway 101 north of San Francisco, take the Alexander Avenue exit and drive one mile (Alexander becomes Bridgeway). Turn right on El Portal and follow to inn. Sausalito is about a twenty-minute (non-rush-hour) drive from San Francisco.

The Inn Above Tide

Sausalito

uilt years ago as a luxury apartment complex, whose residents included Hollywood luminaries like Sam Peckinpah and Clint Eastwood, the three-story, shingled Inn Above Tide sits on pilings directly over San Francisco Bay. A $3.5 million conversion in 1995 created this idyllic overnight destination, whose rooms all offer enchanting panoramic bay and city views. It's arguably the best view of the city you'll find from a Bay Area guest room.

The Red and White Fleet and Golden Gate ferry dock is next door to the inn, and a number of restaurants and nightspots are within walking distance. If the two of you can't tear yourselves away from this romantic environment for dinner, the inn has an arrangement with a local restaurant that will bring supper to your room.

Rooms for Romance

For around $200, the lowest tariff available, you'll have a room with a wonderful bay and city view but without a deck. Deck rooms are available for around $10 more; most of these also have fireplaces. All rooms have a private bath and spa tub for two.

Among the inn's most romantic accommodations are the "Grand Deluxe Rooms" (mid $200 range), which come with a deck, a fireplace, a king-sized bed, and a spa tub for two. The Grand View Deluxe, located on the uppermost level, is a southern corner room offering one of the best views in the house.

If you're feeling flush, indulge yourselves in the Vista Suite (low $400 range), furnished with a draped king-sized bed, a spa tub, a wet bar, and an extended deck positioned to offer an extraordinary view.

All rooms are luxuriously furnished and come equipped with amenities like minibars, refrigerators, robes, and binoculars to enjoy the view. Complimentary wines and cheeses are served each evening.

THE CENTRAL COAST

Daytime Diversions

While everyone has their sights set on the shops of
Carmel, too many folks miss the chance to stroll the
beautiful, white-sand beach along Carmel Bay. Don't
miss it, especially on a sunny day. The beach is only
a short walk from the heart of the village.

In Monterey, Northern California's other Fisherman's
Wharf is crammed with little, open-air markets that dis-
play a variety of fresh catches. These are within walking
distance of the Old Monterey Inn (see listing).

Visitors to Cannery Row's world-famous Monterey
Bay Aquarium shouldn't overlook the paved pedestrian
and bike path that links Cannery Row with Pacific
Grove. Surrey rentals are available along the seaside
path. Despite the sometimes heavy foot and cycle
traffic, it's one of the most romantic promenades you'll
ever take.

Tables for Two

For a fun, convivial atmosphere, drop by the Rio Grill
(California cuisine) in the Crossroads Center off Highway 1 just south of Carmel on Rio Road. Another recommended spot is Fandango's (continental and Basque), 223
Seventeenth Street in Pacific Grove.

Among gourmets, the highest marks go to Fresh
Cream, a critically acclaimed French restaurant in
Monterey's Heritage Harbor near Fisherman's Wharf.
Another good choice for French fare is Melacs at
663 Lighthouse Avenue in Pacific Grove. Gernot's,
649 Lighthouse Avenue, was recommended by more
than one of our innkeeping hosts.

Ventana's highly rated on-site restaurant (see listing;
early reservations advised) is accessible to resort guests
via a winding, romantic path through the Big Sur forest.
Trail-side lights will guide you and other hand-holding
couples back to your rooms after dinner.

OLD MONTEREY INN

500 Martin Street
Monterey, CA 93940
Telephone: (408) 375-8284

Ten rooms and suites, eight with fireplaces. Complimentary full
breakfast served at a large communal table, in the garden, or in
your room. No handicapped access. Smoking is not permitted.
Two-night minimum stay required during weekends; three-night
minimum during holidays. Expensive to deluxe.

Getting There
Monterey is one hundred fifteen miles south of San Francisco
on Highway 1. From Pacific Street near the city's historic section,
head east on Martin Street. The inn is situated in a residential
area and is marked by a small sign on the right side of Martin
Street.

OLD MONTEREY INN

We had a hunch we were in for a treat after the second or third pass along Martin Street searching for the Old Monterey Inn. In our experience, the harder an inn is to find, the more special it is.

Our theory was confirmed when we finally spotted the inn's tiny sign in a tree and entered the wooded property of Gene and Ann Swett, proprietors of what one publication termed one of the most romantic hideaways in the world.

After a short time with Ann, it became obvious why innkeepers and prospective innkeepers from far and wide drop by Old Monterey Inn to learn a thing or two about the business. The level of service and accommodations here would rival most any inn or hotel we've visited. The Swetts have gone the extra mile, and it shows.

The Tudor-style, craftsman estate in which the Swetts raised six children contains ten guest rooms, each with private bath and each offering a different guest experience, thanks to Ann's decorating flourishes. Gene, the resident green thumb, is responsible for the English-style gardens that are in constant color.

Depending on your mood (or the unpredictable Monterey weather), complimentary full breakfast is served either in the impressive dining room, outdoors in the garden, or in your room. Although we'd planned to dine under our warm, down comforter, the morning sun drew us into the garden with several other guests for a memorable breakfast of waffles, whipped cream, and berries.

Rooms for Romance

Tattershall (low $200 range) welcomes guests with its French tapestries and English antiques. There's a luxurious queen-sized bed to warm your hearts and a pretty tiled fireplace to warm your toes.

One of the main house's most private hideaways is Dovecote (low $200 range), the rear-facing, third-floor room decorated in what Ann calls a hunting theme. A fireplace, king-sized bed, window seat, and skylight are among the thoughtful features here.

We were particularly intrigued by Serengeti (mid $200 range), a Carriage House room inspired by Ann's vision of a turn-of-the-century African safari. If you've ever wondered what it's like sleeping under a genuine jungle mosquito net, save the airfare. It's all here, including an authentic safari hat, vintage camera, antique field glasses, and a spa tub for two. A sweet-smelling stash of potpourri sits in an old cigar box.

Our home for a night was the Garden Cottage (mid to high $200 range), a spacious suite with a cozy sitting room, a fireplace, and a step-up bedroom. The shuttered windows filtered an elevated view through limbs of twisting oaks into the garden beyond. Skylights illuminated the entire suite.

Rooms at Old Monterey Inn are well-stocked with thick fluffy towels, toothpaste, and even shaving accessories. Two designer bathrobes hang in the closet. Many rooms have luxurious feather beds.

Spindrift Inn

652 Cannery Row
Monterey, CA 93940
Telephone: (408) 646-8900;
toll-free (800) 841-1879

Forty-two rooms, each with private bath and woodburning fire-place. Half of the rooms have bay views or balconies. Complimentary continental breakfast and morning newspaper delivered to your room. Handicapped access. Smoking is allowed. Two-night minimum stay required during weekends. Expensive to deluxe.

Getting There
From Highway 1, take the Monterey/Aguajito Road exit and drive west. Turn left at Del Monte Avenue and follow signs to Cannery Row. The inn is at the heart of Cannery Row on the bay side of the street.

SPRINDRIFT INN

Monterey

or those expecting to experience John Steinbeck's Cannery Row, a trip down the narrow row during a busy weekend can be a disheartening experience. Tour buses hog the parking lots, tourists clog the streets, and many of the original buildings have been replaced by stucco facades.

At night, however, the picture changes completely. When the cars and tourists leave, the fog sometimes settles in, bringing with it the smells and sounds of the Cannery Row described by Steinbeck. In the early morning, lapping waves and a distant foghorn are all that can be heard. Nights and mornings offer an enchanting taste of what the fabled street must have been like before the tourists came.

Despite its modernization, Cannery Row is still a magical lovers' getaway, especially when savored from the Spindrift Inn. Built on the beach on the site of an old cannery, the inn offers considerable serenity despite its location at the heart of the row.

The inn is just down the street from the Monterey Bay Aquarium and a short jaunt from Fisherman's Wharf. A biking/walking path hugs the coastline connecting the row with quaint Pacific Grove and the wharf.

Rooms for Romance

Although our room faced Cannery Row, we could also see the bay thanks to an expansive set of corner windows. With the exception of the views, the rooms here are similar.

Each one includes a fireplace, a canopied and draped feather bed, and a comforter. A remote-controlled television is hidden in an armoire. The marble baths feature brass fixtures and a second telephone.

Rates at Spindrift Inn range from the high $100 range to the mid $300 range.

GOSBY HOUSE INN

643 Lighthouse Avenue
Pacific Grove, CA 93950
Telephone: (408) 375-1287;
toll-free (800) 527-8828

Twenty-two rooms, twenty with private baths; twelve with fireplaces. Complimentary full breakfast included. Handicapped access.
Smoking is not permitted. Moderate to expensive.

Getting There
From Highway 1, take Highway 68 west to Pacific Grove. Highway
68 becomes Forest Avenue; continue on Forest to Lighthouse
Avenue and turn left; go three blocks to the inn on left.

GOSBY HOUSE INN

Pacific Grove

*I*n our search for peace and quiet, we usually shun hostelries situated at the heart of a town. An exception is Gosby House Inn. Although its location can be described as downtown, this isn't your typical town. Pacific Grove is sleepy compared to its bustling neighbors, Monterey and Carmel. The few businesses along Lighthouse Avenue cater largely to the townsfolk, many of whom reside in tidy Victorians built a hundred years ago.

A Pacific Grove landmark, Gosby House is among the stately structures that have been around since the community's founding as a religious and educational retreat center. In fact, J. F. Gosby, the inn's namesake, opened the Queen Anne–style structure to Pacific Grove's early visitors back in the 1880s.

A full breakfast can be taken with other guests in the parlor of the main house or brought to your room for an extra charge.

Rooms for Romance

It may appear relatively small from the street, but the Gosby House holds twenty-two rooms. All but two of the Gosby's rooms have private baths. Twelve have fireplaces, and most have queen-sized beds. (A handful of rooms have double beds. Make sure to specify

a queen or a king room if you desire one.) The Carriage House rooms, which Mr. Gosby added as business blossomed, feature fireplaces, private balconies, and spa tubs.

The William LaPorte Suite, our Carriage House room for a night, was attached to, but set behind, the main house. The cottage-style room featured country decor, a fireplace, and a sunny, private patio situated off the main path.

Four of the inn's most romantic rooms are situated upstairs in the main house. Their names are Harrison McKinley, Robert Louis Stevenson, Holman, and Gosby. All are offered in the mid $100 range.

Lovers Point (mid $100 range) also has an outside entry with private patio, as well as a fireplace that can be seen from the queen-sized bed.

For lovers on a budget, Gosby House Inn is a bargain. Although you won't pay ocean-view prices (many rooms were in the $100 range at the time of our visit), the coast and the coastal recreation trail is only a short stroll away.

GREEN GABLES INN

104 Fifth Street
Pacific Grove, CA 93950
Telephone: (408) 375-2095

Eleven rooms, six with private baths; six with fireplaces. Complimentary full breakfast served buffet-
style. No handicapped access. Smoking is not
permitted. Moderate to expensive.

Getting There
From Highway 1, take Highway 68 west to Pacific
Grove. Highway 68 becomes Forest Avenue; continue
on Forest Avenue to the beach; and turn right on
Ocean View Boulevard to inn at the corner of Fifth
Street.

GREEN GABLES INN

Pacific Grove

"They don't make 'em like they used to." We don't know who coined the phrase, but he or she must have been describing this sublime place. An architectural show-stopper in its own right, the Green Gables Inn is doubly spectacular given its locale. If the water were any closer, you could fish from your window.

Only a two-lane road separates this lovely half-timbered Victorian from Monterey Bay, and most of the distinctive gabled rooms have dramatic views of the sea or coastline.

Rooms for Romance

Among returning guests, the most-requested room (even though it shares a bath) is Balcony (mid $100 range), on the second floor. One of the particularly appealing attractions of this room, in addition to the ocean view, is the step-down sun porch with daybed. There's no need to draw the drapes for privacy, since neither the adjacent street nor the bike path is visible from your bed. Just enjoy the spectacular view.

Another popular room, Chapel (mid $100 range), features old mahogany, an open-beam ceiling, and step-up window seat. It shares a pair of easily accessible bathrooms with three other rooms.

Jennifer's Room, which does have its own bath with shower, has a huge wall-length window, a window seat, and a brass-and-iron bed.

The huge Lacey Suite is the inn's most expensive accommodation, priced in the mid $100 range. It holds a queen-sized canopied bed, a private bath with antique tub, a huge armoire that covers almost an entire wall, and a sitting room with a gas fireplace. The sitting room and bedchamber are separated by a pretty sliding door. The suite does not have an ocean view and is located directly off the living room.

Elsewhere in the main house is Garrett, which we found a bit too small. It also shares a bath.

While the fairy-tale facade of the main house can prove hard to resist, many guests head for the separate three-level Carriage House, whose rooms (mid $100 range) each have a partial ocean view, a king-sized bed, a gas fireplace, and a private bath. These rooms are spacious but lack the antique charm of the main house.

Whichever room you choose, you'll be greeted by a teddy bear placed somewhere in your chambers.

SEVEN GABLES INN

555 Ocean View Boulevard
Pacific Grove, CA 93950
Telephone: (408) 372-4341

Fourteen rooms, each with private bath and
bay/ocean/coastal view. Complimentary full breakfast
served at large communal table. No handicapped
access. Smoking is not permitted. Two-night minimum
stay required during weekends; three-night minimum
during certain holiday periods. Moderate to deluxe.

Getting There
From Highway 1, take Highway 68 west to Pacific
Grove. Highway 68 becomes Forest Avenue; stay on
Forest Avenue to Ocean View Boulevard and turn
right; follow for two blocks to inn.

SEVEN GABLES INN

Pacific Grove

Arguably California's most beautiful Victorian inn, Seven Gables is the place you've always fantasized about. Relaxing in the front yard on a sunny afternoon, we watched car after car slow to gawking speed as they edged along Ocean View Boulevard past this classic beauty. Even though we were only there for a night, I felt like the guy at the prom with the prettiest girl.

Thanks to the resident Flatley family, those gingerbread-laden, gabled rooms that for years could only be enjoyed from street level can now be savored from the inside. It's true that the stately exterior sets lofty expectations. But the interior is up to the task. The public rooms that greet arriving guests are ostentatious displays of Victoriana, with gilded fixtures, museum-quality antiques, and ornately patterned rugs.

The period theme is carried into the guest rooms, which boast appointments like down-filled couches, inlaid tables and sideboards, antique prints, nine-foot-high armoires, and velvet-covered chairs. Half the inn's rooms are in the main house and half are in the cozy Guest House.

Views from many of the inn's rooms are postcard quality. Although you'll rue the setting of the sun for stealing this scene, the night kicks the other senses into high gear. The smell of the sea and sounds of crashing surf at night lulled us for hours.

Breakfast at Seven Gables, which includes a hot entree, is a convivial, sit-down affair in the inn's ornate dining room.

Rooms for Romance

The most coveted accommodation is Cypress (low $200 range), a Guest House room that boasts a 180-degree view of the ocean and bay. This romantic retreat is appointed with a canopied bed, a large armoire, two antique stained-glass windows, a couch, and a sitting area.

The Gable Room (high $100 range), located on the third floor at the tippity top of the main house, has been enlarged and improved to include a gable and a nice sized bathroom with a shower. The window has been lowered to provide guests with a better view.

The largest of the inn's seven gables is found behind the door of the Bellevue Room (low $200 range), where an elegant chandelier hangs above the sitting area.

Since our last visit, the Carriage House (high $100 range) has been renovated. The one-room cottage has a bay window and window seat overlooking the garden and ocean. It's furnished with a gas fireplace and a canopied bed.

COBBLESTONE INN

Junipero between Seventh and Eighth Avenues
(P.O. Box 3185)
Carmel, CA 93921
Telephone: (408) 625-5222;
toll-free (800) 833-8836

Twenty-four rooms, each with private bath, refrigerator, and gas fireplace. Handicapped access. Smoking is
not permitted. Moderate to expensive.

Getting There
From Highway 1 at Carmel, take Ocean Avenue exit;
turn left on Junipero, two blocks to inn.

COBBLESTONE INN

Carmel

Owned by Four Sisters Inns, the same clan of hoteliers that operates the Gosby House and Green Gables Inns (as well as San Francisco's Petite Auberge and White Swan Inn), the Cobblestone has the same romantic charm that characterizes the other Post-family establishments.

Once upon a time, this was just another plain-Jane motel. But with the addition of a distinctive stone facade, a fresh, new country decor, and other bits of "Carmelization," the Cobblestone has become one of the village's most romantic retreats.

The inn is set in a neighborhood with a mix of homes and businesses, and it's only two blocks from the heart of Carmel village. A walk of about eight blocks will bring you to Carmel's glorious, white-sand beach.

Rooms for Romance

The inn's designated honeymoon suite is room 27, a particularly sunny hideaway (mid to high $100 range) featuring a king-sized, four-poster bed and recessed sitting area under the windows. The bath has a tub-and-shower combination. Only guests staying in this room are treated to breakfast in bed.

Room 26 is another bright room, decked out in the inn's pervasive English country–style theme. But this one is priced more moderately, in the low $100 range. One of the

innkeeper's personal favorites is room 18 (mid to upper $100 range), a sunny corner room with a king-sized bed and a sitting area with a sofa.

The rooms, each equipped with a refrigerator and a gas fireplace, are arranged in a horseshoe shape around a well-tended, slate courtyard dotted with flower planters and small tables.

Ventana

Big Sur, CA 93920

Telephone: (408) 667-2331;

toll-free (800) 628-6500

Fifty-nine rooms and suites, each with private bath, refrigerator, and videocassette player; forty-nine with fireplaces; twelve with private outdoor spas. Complimentary continental breakfast and afternoon wine and cheese. Restaurant, pools, sauna, Japanese-style baths, fitness center, spa services, and on-site store. Handicapped access. Smoking is allowed. Two-night minimum stay required during weekends; three-night minimum during holiday periods. Deluxe.

Getting There

Ventana is 28 miles south of the last traffic light in Carmel just off coastal Highway 1. The drive from Monterey takes about forty-five minutes.

VENTANA

Big Sur

Granted, the sight and sound of surf breaking just outside your window is pretty special, especially to big-city folk. But there's nothing like a fifty-mile, tree-and-sea view from high above the ocean to test one's sensual limits.

Encouraged by a couple of friends who termed Ventana a "hedonistic hideaway," we booked a room to celebrate a special birthday. Until that time, our encounters with Big Sur were primarily on four wheels as we savored the coastal beauty along Highway 1. As pleasant as those visits were, we didn't fully appreciate this region until we sampled Ventana. The inn is as spectacular as its setting.

Ventana's fifty-nine guest rooms are spread among some 240 acres in a dozen single- and two-story units of weathered cedar. Accommodations are connected by foot paths that wind through a mountain meadow ringed by redwood, oak, and bay laurel trees. Another foot path, romantically lit at night, leads through the forest to the renowned Ventana restaurant a short stroll away.

Because of the privacy-sensitive layout of the complex (not to mention the indoor entertainment options), you're likely to feel alone, even when the inn is booked solid. The largest gathering of guests is often found in the late afternoon, sampling a sumptuous, complimentary wine-and-cheese buffet on the inn's terrace. Continental breakfast is also served communally, but most prefer to dine in bed. Although check-in isn't until 4:30 P.M., Ventana's 1:00 P.M. check-out time is the most generous of all our destinations.

Rooms for Romance

Room 53, The Cottage, is situated at the rear of Ventana's property, overlooking seemingly endless miles of forest. We stayed here and spent much of our time relaxing in our private deck-mounted spa under the highest reaches of a grand oak.

Don't be disappointed that the management won't guarantee a specific room. You really can't go wrong with any of the accommodations here. The most seductive, found in one of the resort's more recent additions, have tiled decks with private hot tubs on the outside and fireplaces inside. Every room has either a balcony or patio and most have ocean vistas.

Rooms are paneled with wood and are decorated in pastel blue, pink, and gold.

Curtained beds with hand-painted headboards and handmade quilts are featured throughout the inn. Accommodations vary from the not-so-standard guest room (starting at just over $200) to spacious fireplace/spa suites (high $400 range), with lots in between.

If an expensive suite is out of reach, you'll still have access to communal Japanese-style hot baths, swimming pool, sauna, and sun deck. Clothing optional areas are also provided.

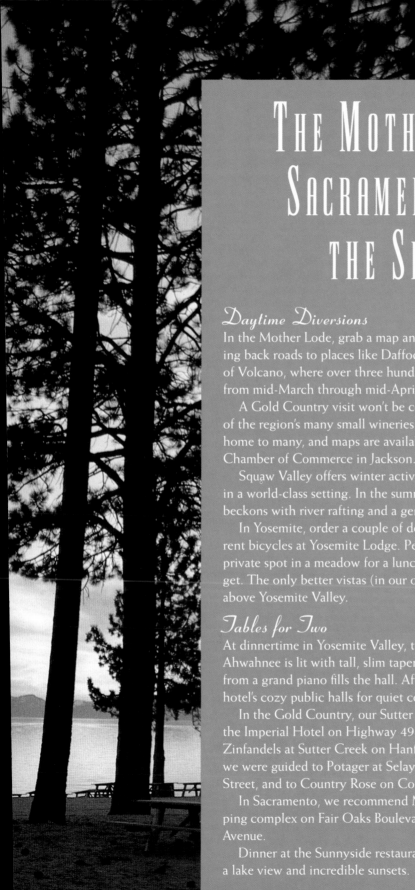

The Mother Lode, Sacramento, and the Sierra

Daytime Diversions

In the Mother Lode, grab a map and find your way along the twisting back roads to places like Daffodil Hill, about three miles north of Volcano, where over three hundred thousand daffodils bloom from mid-March through mid-April.

A Gold Country visit won't be complete without a visit to a few of the region's many small wineries. The Shenandoah Valley is home to many, and maps are available from the Amador County Chamber of Commerce in Jackson.

Squaw Valley offers winter activities like skiing and ice skating in a world-class setting. In the summer, the nearby Truckee River beckons with river rafting and a gentle bike trail.

In Yosemite, order a couple of deli sandwiches in the village and rent bicycles at Yosemite Lodge. Pedal along the many paths to a private spot in a meadow for a lunch with a view you'll never forget. The only better vistas (in our opinion) are from Glacier Point above Yosemite Valley.

Tables for Two

At dinnertime in Yosemite Valley, the grand dining room in the Ahwahnee is lit with tall, slim tapers placed on each table. Music from a grand piano fills the hall. After dinner, retreat to one of the hotel's cozy public halls for quiet conversation and a warm drink.

In the Gold Country, our Sutter Creek innkeepers recommend the Imperial Hotel on Highway 49 in nearby Amador City and Zinfandels at Sutter Creek on Hanford Street. In Nevada City, we were guided to Potager at Selayas and Vlados, both on Broad Street, and to Country Rose on Commercial Street.

In Sacramento, we recommend Mace's, at the Pavilions shopping complex on Fair Oaks Boulevard, and Biba, 2801 Capitol Avenue.

Dinner at the Sunnyside restaurant in Tahoe City comes with a lake view and incredible sunsets.

The Foxes in Sutter Creek

77 Main Street (P.O. Box 159)
Sutter Creek, CA 95685
Telephone: (209) 267-5882

Seven rooms and suites, each with private bath. Complimentary full breakfast cooked to order, served at tables for two or delivered to your room with silver service. No handicapped access. Smoking is not permitted. Two-night minimum stay required during weekends and holiday periods. Moderate to expensive.

Getting There
Sutter Creek is located on Highway 49, just north of the Highway 88 junction, east of Lodi. The inn is located on Highway 49, Sutter Creek's main street.

The Foxes in Sutter Creek

Sutter Creek

Unlike some of the Gold Country's traditional bed-and-breakfast inns, where guests walk on squeaky floors and share a couple of old-style bathrooms, the Foxes treats traveling romantics to a collection of comfortable, well-equipped, nicely decorated rooms, each retrofitted with its own bath.

The Foxes, which was for sale at the time of our last visit, is centrally located in the quaint downtown area of Sutter Creek; shops and restaurants are within easy walking distance.

Rooms for Romance

The Honeymoon Suite (mid $100 range) is among the inn's plushest love nests. It's a spacious room that contains a canopied queen-sized bed, an old-fashioned tub and separate shower, period furniture, two blue velvet wing chairs, and a sitting area with a fireplace. Entry is private, from the porch overlooking the inn's garden.

Romantic travelers should note that the Anniversary Room has a detached bathroom.

Our romantic favorites were some of the rooms found in a separate building behind the main house. The second-floor Garden Room (mid $100 range), which overlooks the tree tops, is decorated in shades of peach, teal, and cream. Two velvet chairs sit before a wood-burning fireplace. The queen-sized bed is partly canopied and side-draped, covered with a down comforter.

Soft grays and blues complement the spacious upstairs Blue Room (mid $100 range), which features a balcony and private entry. Furnishings include an old-fashioned bathtub and separate shower, a pair of French blue leather wing chairs, and antiques.

We were also impressed with the Master Suite (mid $100 range), a spacious downstairs room with a private entry, a separate living room with a fireplace, and a carpeted, skylit bedroom with a queen-sized, half-canopy bed.

The Hideaway, which boasts a large fireplace, is the inn's largest and most private accommodation.

Gold Quartz Inn

15 Bryson Drive
Sutter Creek, CA 95685
Telephone: (209) 267-9155;
toll-free (800) 752-8738

Twenty-four rooms, each with private bath; twenty
with private porches. Complimentary full breakfast
served at tables for two; complimentary afternoon
tea with desserts, appetizers, and other goodies.
Handicapped access. Smoking is not permitted. No
minimum stay requirement. Moderate to expensive.

Getting There
Sutter Creek is located on Highway 49, east of Lodi;
just north of the Highway 88 junction. From Highway
88, turn left onto Highway 49, follow to Bryson Drive
and turn right.

GOLD QUARTZ INN

Sutter Creek

*E*arning three separate entries in our romantic guide to Northern California, the Gold Rush–era burg of Sutter Creek made an obvious impression. We can't imagine any couple driving through this quaint village without stopping for awhile to admire the graceful, old buildings or to visit some of the boutique-style shops that dot Highway 49 downtown. And if you had the foresight to plan an overnighter, there are several cozy alternatives.

Gold Quartz Inn is among the newest, although its Victorian appearance might suggest otherwise. Built only a few years ago, the inn was given a Queen Anne design, typical of many of the town's old buildings and homes. Rooms are bright and spacious, and all have private baths. Rates here begin under $100 and go to the mid $100 range.

Rooms for Romance

Except for some individual styling, rooms 101 and 201 are similarly laid out. Billed as honeymoon suites, each features a carved, four-poster, step-up, king-sized bed. They also contain clawfoot tubs, separate showers, lace curtains, and private porches. These are offered in the mid $100 range.

In the same price range is room 206, one of the inn's most popular. Features include a king-sized bed with brass headboard, a sitting area with two velvet-covered chairs, lace curtains, and a private porch.

Visitors should be aware that Gold Quartz Inn is located just south of downtown Sutter Creek. Consequently, you won't be able to walk to Sutter Creek shops.

Sutter Creek Inn

75 Main Street (P.O. Box 385)
Sutter Creek, CA 95685
Telephone: (209) 267-5606

Eighteen rooms, each with private bath and airconditioning; eleven with fireplaces. Complimentary
full breakfast served at a large communal table. Handicapped access. Smoking is allowed on the porches.
No minimum night stay requirement. Moderate to
expensive.

Getting There
From Highway 99 near Lodi, take Highway 88 to
Highway 49; turn left to Sutter Creek. The inn is
located in town.

Sutter Creek Inn

Sutter Creek

J ane Way, Sutter Creek Inn's longtime proprietress, is a legend among California's bed-and-breakfast innkeepers. When Jane bought the old, Greek revival–style home and opened it to guests more than twenty-five years ago, she created one of the West's first bed-and-breakfast inns. Although the industry has since exploded with competition, Jane and her inn continue to attract a loyal following.

With eighteen guest accommodations (all with their own bathrooms), this is among the Gold Country's largest bed-and-breakfast inns. Rooms are located both in the main house and in private outbuildings.

Sutter Creek Inn features a helping of the antique decor that characterizes the typical bed-and-breakfast, but Jane has sprinkled the rooms with enough of her high-spirited personality to make this place memorable.

Rooms for Romance

A favorite room is the Carriage House, with the unusual feature of his and hers bathrooms. It also has a canopied, queen-sized bed, a sitting area, a tub for two, and a fireplace. The weekend rate is in the mid to upper $100 range.

The Storage Shed (mid to upper $100 range) has a queen-sized swinging bed that hangs from the cathedral ceiling on chains. You'll be able to see the fireplace from the bed, which, by the way, can be stabilized if desired. This room also has a tub for two and a separate shower.

Another swinging bed is found in the Tool Shed (mid $100 range), which is also equipped with a fireplace.

Porch swings overlooking the garden have earned David's Room favored status among returning guests. This elegantly handsome room also has a queen-sized bed, comfortable couch, and fireplace.

Grandmere's Bed-and-Breakfast Inn

449 Broad Street
Nevada City, CA 95959
Telephone: (916) 265-4660

Seven rooms, each with private bath; three with tubs
for two. Complimentary vegetarian breakfast with
hot entree. No handicapped access. Smoking is not
permitted. Two-night minimum stay required during
weekends and holiday periods. Moderate to expensive.

Getting There
From Interstate 80 in Auburn, exit at Highway 49 and
drive about forty-five minutes, following signs to Grass
Valley. Drive past Grass Valley to Nevada City and
exit highway at Broad Street. Turn left and follow to
the top of the hill to inn on left.

GRANDMERE'S BED-AND-BREAKFAST INN

Nevada City

*L*ocated on one of historic Nevada City's narrow streets, this three-story, colonial revival mansion was once the home of Aaron Sargent, who played a major part in the construction of the transcontinental railroad, and his wife, Ellen, who championed women's rights with Susan B. Anthony in the 1860s. Anthony was a frequent guest in the home.

The inn reflects its historic past, from the carriage house beside terraced and closely manicured gardens to the creaky floors and stubborn front door lock. Blond hardwood floors brighten the sitting room, where a sunny window seat and antique furnishings invite guests to curl up with a newspaper and nibble chocolates from a bottomless jar.

A number of such touches hint at the hospitality of innkeepers Doug and Geri Boka. Guests may help themselves to glassware, sodas, magazines, and umbrellas. Spicy tea and three flavors of freshly ground coffee are offered each morning before a hot, meatless breakfast, taken at a communal table or via tray to the garden or your bedroom.

Rooms for Romance

A two-room suite with a private porch entry, the Master Suite (mid $100 range) is the only room with a fireplace, which is surrounded by a sitting area. Oak steps rise to a four-poster, queen-sized bed covered with a white eyelet comforter. Knotty pine paneling encloses the private bath, where a clawfoot tub holds two. A private deck furnished with white wicker chairs overlooks the garden.

Gertie's Room (mid $100 range) has a private garden entrance as well as a kitchen, a sitting area, a queen-sized, white wicker bed, and a private bath with a tub for two.

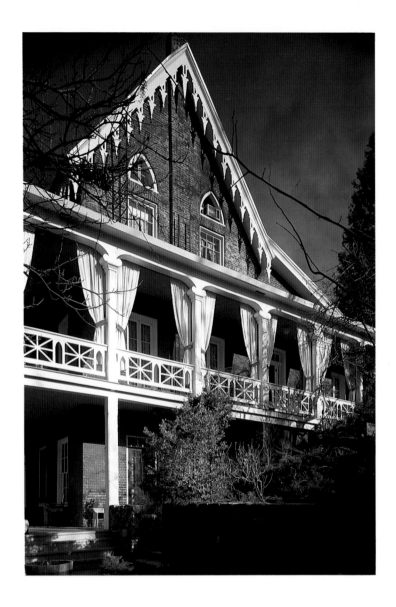

Red Castle Inn

109 Prospect Street
Nevada City, CA 95959
Telephone: (916) 265-5135

Seven rooms and suites, each with private bath. Complimentary multi-
course breakfast served at tables for two or may be taken to your room.
No handicapped access. Smoking is not permitted. Moderate.

Getting There
From Interstate 80 at Auburn, exit at Highway 49 and drive approximately
forty-five minutes to Nevada City. From Highway 49 in Nevada City, exit
at Sacramento Street; take first right on Adams; left on Prospect to inn.

RED CASTLE INN

O ur focus continues to be 'Dwell in the past,' when romance was kindled not by Jacuzzis, VCRs, R-rated films, or other electronic modern stimuli, but rather by the setting and sentimental old-fashioned atmosphere of the grand mansion on the hill," says Red Castle proprietress Mary Louise Weaver. "Our guests are immersed in our nineteenth century style of romance, from the sounds of water gently cascading in the fountains, birds and squirrels in the trees, classical music in the background, to the tiny fairy lights twinkling in the gardens and along the footpaths."

This splendid Gothic revival mansion on Nevada City's Prospect Hill, an architectural landmark from the time of its construction in 1860, was christened the Red Castle by towns-folk, who watched in awe as the stately, four-story brick building took shape.

A century later, the mansion abandoned and sagging, a farsighted admirer stepped in and bought the place. In 1963, a rejuvenated Red Castle (the Smithsonian Institution called it a perfect restoration) became one of California's first bed-and-breakfasts. Rates here are quite reasonable, running from around $100 to the mid $100 range, including a generous breakfast.

By the way, if you're interested in ghost stories, ask Mary Louise or her husband, Conley Weaver, about their encounters with a friendly spirit from the Red Castle's past.

Rooms for Romance

The mansion's builder wasn't simply showing off his wealth when he erected these multistories dripping with Gothic ornamentation. With eleven children to shelter, building such a large house was a practical matter. Today, the children's former tiny bedrooms on the third floor have given way to two suites. The top floor now consists of a two-bedroom suite.

Many honeymooners and anniversary celebrants choose Forest View (mid $100 range) for its curtained and draped canopied bed and the crystal

chandelier on a dimmer control. The bath is tiled and holds a spacious shower frequently used by couples. The room opens to the garden and its own veranda by the fountain.

A high, four-poster bed with a step-up ladder is the centerpiece of Rose Room (low to mid $100 range), whose tall French doors open to a private veranda. From the bed, you can see the town through the trees.

Pictured here is the Garden Room (low $100 range), furnished in mahogany antiques with an Oriental carpet and a canopied bed.

Lap robes are available for evening stargazing near the fountain and koi pond.

McCaffrey House
Bed-and-Breakfast Inn

23251 Highway 108 (P.O. Box 67)
Twain Harte, CA 95383
Telephone: (209) 586-0757

Seven rooms, each with private bath and gas stove.
Complimentary full breakfast served at communal
table, tables for two, or in your bedroom. Communal
spa. No handicapped access. Smoking is not permitted. Two-night minimum stay required during holiday
periods. Moderate.

Getting There
From Sonora, drive east on Highway 108 for eleven
miles. One-half mile past the East Twain Harte
exit, turn right off the highway just beyond the
four-thousand-feet elevation marker. Twain Harte is
approximately three hours by car from the Bay Area.

McCaffrey House Bed-and-Breakfast Inn

Twain Harte

We were just about ready to give up all hope of finding suitably romantic accommodations in the south-central Mother Lode region when we learned about Michael and Stephanie McCaffrey's delightful inn in Twain Harte. If the two of you have never considered a weekend getaway to the Sonora area, a night at McCaffrey House is reason enough to pack your bags.

The inn's setting is a wooded hollow at the edge of the Stanislaus National Forest. The McCaffreys used to vacation here in a country cottage that's since been replaced by this attractive three-story inn with its expansive windows, decks, and balconies.

The community of Twain Harte is near the Dodge Ridge ski area and lovely Pinecrest Lake. Columbia State Historic Park is not far away.

Rooms for Romance

In addition to a private bath, each country pine–furnished room has a videocassette player and a gas stove controlled by a timer, so you can drift off to sleep without having to get up and turn off the fire. All the beds, which are triple-sheeted, are covered with quilts made by the Amish of Lancaster County, Pennsylvania.

For traveling romantics, the third-floor rooms described below can't be beat. The Burgundy Room (around $100) faces the forest at the rear of the property. Furnishings include a queen-sized sleigh bed made of pine and iron. A dimmer next to the bed controls the mood lighting.

Facing the side and back is the Evergreen Room (around $100), which has a queen-sized sleigh bed and offers a lovely view from the small balcony reached through French doors. In the True Blue Room (around $100), French doors open to a small deck facing the side yard.

THE STERLING HOTEL

1300 H Street
Sacramento, CA 95814
Telephone: (916) 448-1300;
toll-free (800) 365-7660

Twelve rooms, each with private bath and dual Jacuzzi tub.
Restaurant. Handicapped access. Smoking is not permitted.
Moderate to deluxe.

Getting There
Lettered streets intersect numbered streets in downtown Sacramento.
The hotel is at the intersection of Thirteenth and H Streets.

THE STERLING HOTEL

Sacramento

When Richard Kann unveiled his grand plans to create a small, luxury hotel from a downtown Sacramento Victorian boardinghouse, more than a few scoffed. How fortunate for us that he persevered. But he did more than just persevere. Not only did he make believers of his skeptics, but even Kann's supporters were surprised by the results.

The transformation, which required more than a little fairy dust, is extraordinary. While the Sterling incorporates most every contemporary comfort possible, the Victorian integrity of the building has been preserved. It's probably the finest small luxury hotel in inland Northern California.

With its convenient location, within three blocks of the state capitol, the Sterling is popular among visiting business types. However, it's also favored among visiting twosomes attracted by the romantic ambience and certain special touches. You see, this quaint establishment claims to be the only hotel in the nation to offer private, oversized Jacuzzis in each room.

Rooms for Romance

On the hotel's second floor, room 202 (low $200 range) is often requested by couples. It faces the side of the property and is furnished with a beautiful wood-canopied, queen-sized bed that sits before a large window. The spacious bathroom has pink tile and stained-glass windows. A pedestal sink and brass fixtures grace this and each of the other rooms. Each is

also furnished with a large deck.

Room 304 is the bright, prominent corner bay room and one of the hotel's most popular. Next door in room 303 (high $100 range), there's a balcony that overlooks magnolia trees in the front. This is a spacious room with an Oriental carpet and one of the hotel's largest Jacuzzi tubs.

Room 302 (low $100 range), set at the back of the building on the third floor, is the smallest— and possibly the coziest—room in the house.

PlumpJack Squaw Valley Inn

1920 Squaw Valley Road (P.O. Box 2407)
Olympic Valley, CA 96146
Telephone: (916) 583-1576;
toll-free (800) 323-7666

Sixty rooms, each with private bath. Swimming pool, hot tubs, and restaurant.
Handicapped access. Smoking is allowed in some rooms. Three-night minimum
stay required during holiday periods. Deluxe.   Two ok

Getting There
From Interstate 80 in Truckee, take the Highway 89 exit and follow the highway
toward Tahoe City. Drive ten miles and turn right on Squaw Valley Road. Follow
for two miles to the ski area. Inn is on right across the street from the tram.

PLUMPJACK SQUAW VALLEY INN
Olympic Valley

This elegant Sierra inn has come a long way since its creation in the 1940s as a no-frills overnight lodge for winter sports enthusiasts. In 1960, it served a stint as a dormitory for delegates to the 1960 Olympic Games at Squaw Valley. Renovated in the mid 1990s, PlumpJack Squaw Valley Inn has been transformed into an elegant small hotel that's one of the most romantic destinations in the North Lake Tahoe area.

The inn is named after Jack Falstaff, a life-loving character from Shakespeare's plays. In keeping with the name, the interior decor is theatrical, featuring whimsical metal sculpture and bold architecture. The owners also operate other Northern California PlumpJack dining and wine establishments.

For skiers, the two-story shingled inn couldn't be more conveniently located. It's almost directly under the Squaw Valley gondola that transports visitors to the ski area and to an upper elevation resort area that includes a year-round ice skating rink. In addition to skiing and ice skating, bungee jumping, indoor wall climbing, bicycling, and horseback riding are among other pursuits available at Squaw Valley.

Rooms for Romance

Guest rooms have a contemporary, clean look, and are equipped with a king-sized bed or two queen-sized beds. Appointments include video cassette players (there's also a tape library), hooded bathrobes, down comforters, and hair dryers. Rates from spring through fall are in the mid $100 range, jumping to the low $200 range in the winter. If you're splurging, consider a one-bedroom suite with a spa tub (around $400).

Guests have access to a swimming pool and communal whirlpool tubs.

Ahwahnee Hotel

Yosemite Village
Yosemite National Park, CA 95389
Telephone: (209) 252-4848

One hundred and twenty-three hotel and cottage
rooms, each with private bath. Swimming pool,
restaurant, tennis court, and lounge. Handicapped
access. Smoking is allowed in some rooms. Deluxe.

Getting There
The hotel is located in Yosemite Valley near the village. From Highway 99 at Merced, follow Highway
140 (Yosemite exit) through Mariposa to the park.

AHWAHNEE HOTEL

Yosemite National Park

$\mathcal{I}$f one were to list the man-made wonders of California, Yosemite's Ahwahnee Hotel would be assured a spot. Its location alone would place it near the top. This magnificent wood-and-stone fortress, dwarfed by the sheer granite cliffs of the Royal Arches, is probably the most dramatically situated (and popular) hotel in all of California.

Five thousand tons of stone were used in constructing this plush, six-story structure, which opened in 1927. Seven cottages containing twenty-two bedrooms were added the next year. Rates during those early days were $15 to $20 per night.

Although nightly tariffs now start in the low $200 range, the Ahwahnee continues to pack 'em in. Calling even one year in advance still might not guarantee you a room reservation during a peak period. But set foot in this awe-inspiring hotel and you'll immediately understand why. A timeless Native American theme (combined with some Art Deco flourishes) permeates the hotel, and the public spaces are spacious and inviting. Of particular note is the cavernous dining room with an open-raftered ceiling and peeled, sugar-pine log trusses. More than a dozen floor-to-ceiling windows afford spectacular views. We enjoyed a particularly romantic Valentine's Day dinner here while snow fell outside and sounds of a Steinway echoed through the hall.

One of the Ahwahnee's prime attractions is the annual Bracebridge Dinner, a Renaissance Christmas feast and musical celebration. So popular is this event that you have to win a lottery to attend. It's a long shot, at best, as some sixty thousand people annually compete for the opportunity to break bread with Squire Bracebridge in medieval splendor.

Rooms for Romance

Because of the very high occupancy rate here, it's difficult—but not impossible—to reserve a specific room.

Rooms 230, 232, and 234, where balconies afford a 180-degree vista from El Capitan to Half Dome, comprise what is known as the Presidential Suite (President Kennedy overnighted here). Alas, they must be booked together ($600 range), so you'll need to bring along friends or family.

Room 417 is the only king-bedded room with its own balcony. Room 118, called the El Dorado Room (upper $200 range), is considered a junior suite and has a spa tub in the bathroom. For a more woodsy experience, many guests prefer the Ahwahnee's upscale cottages, which offer a charm unique in the valley. Cottages 714 and 719 have fireplaces and king-sized beds. Because the cottages have no air-conditioning in the summer, and because they are a slushy stroll away from the main hotel building in the winter, we recommend these units only for fall and spring getaways.

Appendix

More Travel Resources for Incurable Romantics

More Weekends for Two in Northern California: 50 All-New Romantic Getaways
Weekends for Two in Southern California: 50 Romantic Getaways
Weekends for Two in the Pacific Northwest: 50 Romantic Getaways
Weekends for Two in the Southwest: 50 Romantic Getaways
Weekends for Two in New England: 50 Romantic Getaways

Each richly illustrated with more than 150 color photos, these books by Bill Gleeson are the definitive travel guides to the country's most romantic destinations.

Free Travel Updates

We continue to discover new romantic destinations and reevaluate our currently featured inns and small hotels, and we're happy to share this information with readers. For a free update on our new discoveries and recommendations (and new books in the *Weekends for Two* series), visit the Chronicle Books Web Site at www.chronbooks.com or send a stamped, self-addressed business-sized envelope to Bill Gleeson, Weekends for Two Update, Chronicle Books, 85 Second Street, Sixth Floor, San Francisco, CA 94105. We always appreciate hearing about your own romantic discoveries as well!

Index

CAST YOUR VOTE!

Northern California's Most Romantic Hotel or Inn

Complete and mail to Bill Gleeson, Weekends for Two, Chronicle Books, 85 Second Street, Sixth Floor, San Francisco, CA 94105. Enclose a stamped, self-addressed business-sized envelope if you'd like a response or a free travel update.

Our favorite Northern California romantic retreat (does not have to be featured in this book):

_____

Name of hotel/inn

_____

City/Town

What makes this place special:

_____

_____

_____

_____

_____

Signed (addresses/names are not for publication):

_____

I have no connection with the operators of this property.